I0475033

INVESTING IN RENTAL PROPERTIES FOR BEGINNERS

CREATE WEALTH AND PASSIVE INCOME WITH INTELLIGENT BUY THROUGH REAL ESTATE INVESTING (BUY, REHAB, RENT, REINVESTED)

By

THOMAS LEE

TABLE OF CONTENTS

WHY YOU NEED THIS BOOK

As far as investing in rental properties is concerned, it is one type of investment that has continued to generate more interest than ever imagined. Buying of homes has ceased to be just finding a good home for yourself; it has become a means of making good income as long as you know your way around as an investor. Formerly, it was all about buying stocks and bonds but presently, a lot of wise investors have looked beyond their noses and seen that beyond buying a good home, real estate can be a lucrative and reliable investment in comparison to other sources of income they might have.

Now I know I have gotten your 'radars' up and you would want to know most of the necessities of investing in real estate. Let's talk about rental property. This is a type of investment where you buy a property and rent out same to one or more tenants. Therefore, it is necessary you know that being the landlord, it is exclusively your duty to pay the mortgage, related taxes and over all cost of maintaining the said building. In order to cover all these expenses and make a little profit, especially while you are still paying the mortgage, you should be able to charge a reasonable rent. After the payment of the mortgage is completed, you will begin to enjoy maximized profit from your investment.

Still on investing in rental properties, you should also know that the more you take care of your building, the higher the chances of such property appreciating over the years thereby leaving the investor with an asset that is worth more in the real estate market. This does not mean there are no downsides to investing in this particular market. For example, you might end up having a bad tenant who has no maintenance culture and within a short period, you find your property damaged which leaves you with more expenses than necessary. There is also a situation where the building lies dormant for a long time because there is no tenant. In this case, the monthly cash flow you are left with is nothing but negative since you will end up making the monthly mortgage payments from your pocket or another source.

In order to enjoy the most of the investment, especially as a first time homebuyer, it is strongly advised that you buy properties that are situated in areas that are known to experience very low vacancy rates. Also, you should consider the type of individuals you rent your property to so that you don't end up spending money every now and then on repairs which are easily avoidable if you have good tenants. You should be mentally and physically prepared for the responsibilities of being a landlord and in a case where you don't see yourself fit for all it entails, then you should consider getting the services of a professional property manager who bears these responsibilities on your behalf, for a price though.

INTRODUCTION

I s it possible to make money investing in real estate? You see all of those ads for courses that cost hundreds of dollars, and claim to teach you how to make money by investing in real estate. The truth is that some research and knowledge can save you hundreds, and even thousands, when you invest in rental property. If you have some money to invest, rental property is a great way to turn your money into a lifetime of income.

There are many advantages to investing in rental property, but there are a few disadvantages as well. One advantage is that it is a long term investment that in the past has given an annual rate of return at around nine or ten percent. This is comparable to the stock market, but with significantly less risk. The capital gains tax on any profit you make from your rental property is twenty eight percent, which is less than most investment or employment income. One of the disadvantages of investing in rental property is the cost of tenant repairs, and another is vacancies.

There are some tips to follow to maximize the return on your rental property investment. The first is to consider a month to month lease for your rental property. Most landlords prefer to rent for a fixed period of time, like six months or one year. The advantages are less vacancy and more stability. There are some disadvantages to having a longer lease time as well. One is that it takes much longer to get an unwanted tenant out due to the legal system. With a month to month lease you are only required to give a tenant one month of notice to have them move. Certain groups of people, like college students and workers who may be relocated among others, actually prefer a short term month to month lease, and these groups will usually not sign an agreement for an extended time.

A short month to month lease can actually save you money in your real estate investing. This is because it is easier and quicker to raise the rent if your expenses for upkeep and other costs go up. With a longer lease, you can not raise the rent for that length of time, even if your costs go up. With a month to month lease, if your costs go up, you only have to give the tenant one month of notice before you can charge them more.

CHAPTER 1
TAP YOUR CREATIVE MIND POWER FOR PROBLEM SOLVING

The difference between the big winners in life and almost everyone else is in their ability to solve problems. You can be one of these big winners, too! Like them, you came into this world equipped with the innate power to solve these problems. You just have to learn to tap creative mind power to deal with all your problems successfully.

Our subconscious mind, the seat of our emotions and the creative mind, is the key to everything. If you will be able to tap creative mind power, you will be able to control it to your infinite good. The fact is, it is possible for you to program and orientate your mental computer to handle any problem that may ever come your way.

When we focus on our problems, the preoccupation with them magnifies them to proportions immensely greater than they are in reality. When we tap creative mind power to find a solution, then the problem will be solved. It may take time to solve our problems, and the solutions may not exactly be comfortable or pleasurable. In fact, good solutions often require you to invest extra effort in implementing them. But when you utilise your creative mind power, you find that good solutions are just there all the while.

Geniuses, such as Sir Isaac Newton and Thomas Edison, learned how to use the power of their creative minds. According to the official biographer of Sir Isaac Newton, the great mathematician and physicist had a peculiar gift: he possessed the ability to hold a problem continuously in his mind until he had had seen it through. This great scientist knew all problems had solutions; he also knew that all he needed to reach a solution was the power of his creative mind.

Thomas Edison shared the same mindset. The incredible amount of persistence he showed in his quest to invent the electric light bulb is the stuff of legend. But despite the obstacles, he was never fazed because he was always convinced that the problem had a solution.

You can learn to tap creative mind power and become a genius. Or, you can, at least, function like a genius. The potential to become one is there. There are techniques that help you harness your innate creative abilities to demolish any problem you will ever face. It can never be said often enough: you have within you the ability and the power to solve every problem.

When you have internalized this conviction that you can overcome any problem, then you will have reached the starting point on the road to a successful life. Problems will always come, but you can solve them every time, once you have learned to tap creative mind power.

CHAPTER 2
CREATIVE WAYS TO MAKE MONEY - UNLEASH THE MONEY MACHINE IN YOUR HEART!

C reative ways to make money: You have a money machine inside of your mind. It's time to use it. The internet can be your primary tool, but not necessarily. Pablo Picasso once remarked, "The chief enemy of creativity is "good" sense."

If you want the same old results, just keep thinking the same old way. The World Wide Web is an incredibly huge market and it is free to all. It is especially inviting to those who seek creative ways to make money. One thing to keep in mind when you think of making money is how much will you have to invest and how large is the risk? So conventional wisdom went, anyway.

No longer is it required to risk rack and ruin to start a business, whether it is a new type or something along old, familiar lines. If you have ever wanted to use your creativity to make money, the time has never been better. What are some of the creative ways to make money? All of these are a heck of a lot easier if you go on the internet. Here are 9 to get you started:

You can create and sell your own unique version of plans, patterns or software for something you enjoy. Anything from stuffed bunnies to experimental aircraft.

You can be a sales representative for something you love, but couldn't afford to do. As an example, if you love Mercedes Benz cars, but could never afford one, you can become an affiliate for a dealer and never have to leave home to sell your beauties.

You can write your own eBook and sell it. You can also sell other peoples' ebooks.

Love old books? Start a web site on collecting, pricing, buying, restoring and storing old and rare books. You can also write and sell your own ebooks on old books!

You can become a commission internet salesperson for companies like Amazon.(You can actually do this with anything: hospital medical equipment, asphalt plants, bulldozers. Anything can be sold from a web site).

You can create your own online bookstore using Amazon and other companies without even putting up a shelf.

You can create your own brand of children's birthday party ideas and items.

You can become an online consultant on anything you are well versed in.

If there is an unusual hobby you have, it might be possible to create a profitable web site about it. For example, I know a lady who does well with a site involving just antique china dolls.

The list goes on and on when it comes to creative ways to make money, but I think you get the idea. Where to start? Right now, you should feel like a kid set loose in a candy shop on a shopping spree. Taking your time and learning the ropes properly, you can create multiple streams of income all revolving around your creativity, talents and interests. It doesn't get any better than this, folks.

It will take work and patience, however. On the other hand, if you are doing something you love, long hours and setbacks won't seem like work, will they? Oh, did I mention that you should go after something you love to do? For the first time in your life, you are being encouraged to pursue just what you ove, not what someone else thinks will sell or will be popular or in demand in the future.

Edwin Land (The creator of the Polaroid camera) said, "An essential aspect of creativity is not being afraid to fail. Every creative act is a sudden cessation of stupidity."

Choose something you love to do and the ideas will flow freely. If you are attracted to a really small niche where there are not that many people interested, that's perfectly alright. There are ways to get others with the same interest to gather around you, to become followers of yours. You can sell to and create with these people. They will have new ideas for you to examine, get excited about and to incorporate into your business.

Taking your time, you will find that almost everything mentioned here is free. There are many places like Squidoo.com and HubPages.com that let you create a website with them free.

Don't know how? They have excellent tutorials and they, also, are free. Creative ways to make money: How far can you count? How happy do you want to be? You are free to create anything you want. There is cheap software that allows you to make your own videos and put them on the internet. You're a plumber and love the work? Set up a plumbing information expert site.

CHAPTER 3
HOW TO EMBRACE FRUSTRATION AS THE KEY TO CREATIVITY

Frustration is the foundation to creativity and the birthplace of new insights.

You may try to ignore the struggle that frustration throws up, though if embraced, the battle allows you to form a new relationship with the creative process.

Resistance stifles creativity since you become embroiled in negative emotions that inhibit genius and wisdom.

In one way, you are enslaved to the emotion, but not the intoxicating highs that go with it.

Learn to live with tension to harness inspiration, as alternative medicine advocate Deepak Chopra states: "Be comfortable with and embrace paradox, contradiction, and ambiguity. It is the womb of creativity."

It is important to reframe your relationship with frustration if you seek to move deeper into creativity.

This doesn't mean you should enjoy it, though

acceptance goes a long way to be able to benefit from its power.

Frustration is obvious in the countless rejection letters you receive in reply to your book submission or the "D" on your mid-term paper. Whilst you despise it, you accept there is something to be gained, otherwise you wouldn't be frustrated.

Many people have an ambivalent relationship with frustration - in fact one that inhibits creativity. They welcome the inspiration that sparks new ideas. However, they feel frustrated when it does not play out according to plan.

"If you want to be an artist of any sort, it seemed to me, then handling your frustration is a fundamental aspect of the work - perhaps the single most fundamental aspect of the work. Frustration is not an interruption of your process; frustration is the process," affirms the acclaimed author Elizabeth Gilbert in: Big Magic: Creative Living Beyond Fear.

Some people experience flashes of creativity and inspiration one day, and resistance the next.

The key to inspiration lies somewhere in the middle, when you are open to the unknown.

In the unconscious your greatest accomplishments

emerge, since you are not bound by expectations other than the flow of inspiration.

Expand Your Horizons

Working with frustration requires being acquainted with its energy. You recognise how it occupies space in your body and the tension that arises. These are the boiling points for creative success.

"People need trouble - a little frustration to sharpen the spirit on, toughen it. Artists do; I don't mean you need to live in a rat hole or gutter, but you have to learn fortitude, endurance. Only vegetables are happy," states the late American writer William Faulkner.

Collaborating with frustration means being aware of what is being called forth. If you exploit it correctly, you will channel creativity into the tip of a ballpoint pen.

Frustration is a sign you have reached a plateau. The subconscious mind advises you to step out of the known, to give creativity a home in which to flourish.

That's why you should welcome frustration as a source of wisdom.

It is the intuitive part of you summoning to reach deeper into the abyss of your mind and expand your horizons.

Frustration invites you to be less invested in outcomes and to channel creativity through your core.

Rest if you must when you reach a sticking point and engage in something non-creative, meaningless and devoid of intent. A valve releases pressure for gas to escape and so should you.

The English economist Tim Harford states in a TED Talk titled: How Frustration Can Make Us More Creative: "These distractions were actually grists to their creative mill. They were able to think outside the box because their box was full of holes."

Awaken Your Creative Impulses

As someone who has been involved in the arts my entire life, I recognise the call of frustration and use it wisely.

I enjoy being active and engage in exercise when frustration calls. Aside from the release of endorphins, I am receptive to new sources of inspiration and no longer attached to an idea whose time has passed.

In the same way, be mindful of your sleep and avoid burning the midnight oil to get more work completed.

Nutrition and hydration are important too. I have eliminated consumption of packaged and junk foods over time which helped my mind flourish with new ideas. I nurture my body and mind with the attentiveness it deserves. I am creating a home for creativity to reside so it feels welcomed.

Remember; frustration is a sign post calling you to examine parts of the creative process that require change. Think of travelling down a freeway that will take you so far, before having to choose a new road. You are only as good as your recent creative endeavour. Awaken your creative impulses and don't allow yourself to become stagnant.

CHAPTER 4
INVESTING IN RENTAL PROPERTIES FOR BEGINNERS - BUILDING A SOLID RESIDUAL INCOME

This chapter is an informative guide to investing in rental properties for beginners.

There are many ways to make money in real estate, but investing in rental properties is by far the most lucrative, offering investors a twofold investment return; a steady residual income from the monthly rental and the equity from the property itself. Building wealth from rental property investments should not be taken lightly though; there are many things to consider before you purchase your first property. Here is a practical guide to investing in rental properties for beginners.

Look for properties that will require little or no repairs to get it ready to rent, down time means you will have no income from the property until it is rented. It is also important to use a balance sheet for each property that you intend to rent, this will show you how much you have invested in the purchase and repairs with the amount of return you can expect once the property is rented. Every detail of your investment strategy should be well planned with attention to the day to day management and maintenance as well as rental contracts. It is a good idea to also have a list of qualified repairmen to handle any potential emergency situation. You should also research the area you plan to rent in. Knowing the personal and financial climate of the area will give you valuable information to help you determine if the location is right for you.

Properties in popular seasonal locations have the potential for higher rental rates and could also be rented weekly. Another great rental investment idea is business property, rental rates are almost always higher for this type of property and most rentals of this type require a long-term commitment. Consider each possible rental property you view with its overall potential for quick profit, and ask yourself; is this an ideal location for such a property? How quickly can this property be ready to rent? What is the total amount I will need to invest, and what is return amount on my investment?

If you plan on purchasing your first rental property with a loan, then you will need to develop a spread sheet for the property you intent to purchase. A typical spreadsheet will cover a 12-month time line and include all income and expenses for the property; most of this information can be found in your personal balance sheet you created for the property. Along with your spreadsheet you will need to have a business plan that outlines your proposal to purchase and maintain your rental property. Your business plan should include the type of property you plan to rent, how you intend to manage and maintain your property and be sure to include any information that shows your ability to be profitable; a popular seasonal location or high traffic business or commercial property or other rental property with a high profit potential. You will also need to include how you intend to overcome any potential obstacles. Investing in rental properties for beginners is a lucrative means to achieving a long term residual income.

CHAPTER 5
INVESTING IN RENTAL PROPERTY FOR BEGINNERS - 7 TIPS FROM A SEASONED INVESTOR

There is so much hype around investing in rental property that makes it sound too easy for beginners. Investing in real estate is a proven method to build wealth, but it is a long term deal. A novice real estate investor should consider joining a real estate investment club to get the scoop on what it really takes to manage rental property.

Investing in rental property is not a get rich quick operation. It is a long term commitment that includes responsibility. Even with a property manager, if you can find a good one, there are accounting and fiscal responsibilities to consider. Here are some tips from a seasoned pro:

1. Start out with just one rental property and learn the ropes.

2. Decide what kind of tenants you are willing to deal

with.

3. Allow for at least a 10% vacancy rate.

4. Be realistic about potential maintenance expenses.

5. Don't force your first deal. Keep looking until a profitable investment opportunity presents itself.

6. Don't buy property far away.

7. Don't assume that you will be able to get a good property manager. Trust me on this one.

As time goes by and you gain experience, buying property in different areas will be more realistic because you will know in advance what problems may occur. Even if your goal is to hire property managers, ultimately you need to be able to take responsibility for your real estate investment. Over time, rents should rise and your mortgage debt will decrease if managed properly. Remember, rental property is long term deal but it is one of the few proven paths to financial independence.

CHAPTER 6
THE TRUTH ABOUT REAL ESTATE INVESTING FOR BEGINNERS

As a new real estate investor, you don't know anything about anything. It is so easy for you to be taken for your money. Many of you will take heed to this chapter and many of you will not. For those of you that listen, I can save you a ton of pain, headaches, and money.

The first thing new investors need to do is set up their business properly. That means setting up an LLC, an office in your home to start, and getting your business cards. The most important thing I want you to get out of this is that real estate investing is a real business.

It's not something you just try out or talk about in the water cooler. The stakes are high, and you could lose your shirt, shoes, and savings.

You must complete your plan and stick to it. If not, you can easily get thrown off track by anyone. You should also set your 90 day goals, as well as your 6 month and one year goals. It is very important to have an education budget that includes a REIA membership, and a mentor/coach.

Try to find someone who is successful in the niche that you want to invest in.

Make sure that your mentor is actively doing deals and they are not just telling you to do some theory B.S. that they have learned. It is critical to your success that you take A-C-T-I-O-N while you are excited about your new career.

Without action, all of your reading and talking will be in vain. Most newbies get caught up in what we call analysis of paralysis. If you surround yourself with wise counsel, you won't have to worry about screwing up. You will make mistakes, it is just part of the learning curve.

Keep in mind that a person who is actively doing deals probably won't give you his time for FREE! Pay your mentor and they will take care of you. It's a part of the game so just accept it. One day, you will be the teacher helping the student.

I don't recommend starting out in the rehabbing niche as a new investor. There are simply to many things that can go wrong. You don't want to be in a position where you go broke or lose your confidence on your first deal.

Wait until you have more experience before you start

dealing with contractors and hard money lenders. A rehab deal could look like a winner from the outside but one unexpected "problem" can quickly take you over your budget.

I will educate you on the best strategies that a new investor should choose that requires some money, but not a ton of money. Please don't believe the hype about "no money down" investing. You always have to use money. It just doesn't have to be yours. I advise you to have a little nest egg when getting started.

CHAPTER 7
INVESTING IN RENTAL PROPERTIES FOR BEGINNERS - THE 5 ABSOLUTELY ESSENTIAL THINGS TO KNOW!

I f you are considering becoming a landlord, then you are about to embark on an epic journey. Investing in rental properties for a beginner can be the best decision that they ever make or it can be a catastrophic nightmare.

Get educated- The number one reason that most novice property investors end up losing money is because they did not get themselves the right property education in the first place. In this World of immediate gratification and wanting everything on a plate, most people approach property investing in the same way. This is a big mistake. Property investing involves you taking on huge amounts of debt and so education should be your number one priority. If you are short of cash and can't pay to get educated you can find many sources of free information about property investing on the Internet.

Assume the worst - There are a lot of very greedy people involved in property that will take your money off you quicker than you can blink and give you nothing in return. In any industry where you are talking about huge amounts of money being spent on deals, you are going to get the vultures who hang around trying to bleed you dry. Be on your guard and don't trust anyone blindly, make people work to gain your trust.

Learn how to do the maths - It doesn't matter if you where useless at maths in high school. if you want to succeed as a property investor or developer, you need to learn a little about sums now. Working out things like rental yield and return on investment are going to be essential to your success.

Research, research and then research some more - This is perhaps the most important thing. You need to research everything, from what location to investing, what type of properties to buy, what sort of finance to use, who is the best solicitor around, to who are the best workmen to hire. These are just a few of the things you need to research to insure that things run smoothly and that you are not over paying for anything and that you get the best people for the job.

Get yourself a mentor - Investing in rental properties for beginners can be a nightmare, if you want to progress quicker and reduce the mistakes you make, then you will need to get yourself a mentor. This doesn't have to be someone that you pay lots of money to, it can be someone you connect with on a property forum whose free advice you follow. A website can also act as a mentor if it has valuable advice to help you succeed.

CHAPTER 8
INVESTING IN RENTAL PROPERTIES FOR BEGINNERS - YOU WON'T BE A BEGINNER FOR LONG

Here are some tips for investing in rental properties for beginners. Your first couple of transactions may be nerve-wracking but if you keep your head and don't let your emotions get in the way, you may be successful from the start. Soon you won't need to read about investing in rental properties for beginners, you'll be a pro.

This may sound like a no-brainer but your main goal is to make a profit. Profit can be achieved based on a combination of different things that you can do.

As a beginner, when investing in rental properties, you want to make sure you are well organized. This can truly be the difference between making money and not.

1. If you're going to create a company to keep things

separate, do it first before you start the buying process. It'll be more difficult to move the property to a company later than to buy it under that company initially.

2. Keep accurate records from the start. You can't know how much money you're making or what you need if you're not keeping up with your expenses. A bank or other investor will want to know exactly what type of finances you have and will need.

3. You need to have an accurate account of the money needed to purchase the property, the down payment, closing costs, repair costs, etc. Be prepared if it will be some time before the property is ready for tenants. You will have to pay the monthly mortgage until it is rented.

4. Keep a projected financial balance sheet. Have accurate estimates of monthly income and expenses for each property. Don't just guess. Research rental property in the area.

Being well organized is probably the biggest tip for investing in rental property for beginners. It will make every transaction much easier and more profitable. The research and effort that you put in from the start will make a big difference.

CHAPTER 9
INVESTING IN RENTAL PROPERTY - KEY FACTS TO CONSIDER

B efore investing in rental property, it is always wise to do a little homework and pre-planning. Such actions on your part can substantially improve the likelihood that your resulting rental property investment will be successful. The following are some key elements that every careful investor should investigate and consider before purchasing rental property and becoming a landlord.

1.   Location, Location, Location - This is a familiar slogan in the real estate world. The location of a rental property plays a large role in the supply, or demographics, of tenants who are available to rent the property. It only makes sense to purchase properties located in areas where you'd be comfortable in dealing with the general population living there. Location also plays a significant role in the market value of a property, and its future appreciation potential. Properties that are located in poor

or decaying areas will not have the long-term market value appreciation potential as properties that are located in better neighborhoods.

2. Condition of Property - A low-priced bargain "fixer upper" investment property, while looking attractive on the surface, can turn into an expensive money pit to make the necessary repairs and upgrades. One reason is that neglected properties in poor condition commonly have "hidden defects" that must first be corrected before the planned upgrades can be made. For these types of properties, not only must the additional renovation costs be absorbed, but also the "lost rent" opportunity cost must be factored in. In this respect, purchasing a more expensive and reliable "turn key" rental property that is in good condition may actually turn out to be a better overall investment.

3. Price and Financing - Knowing the actual fair market price of an investment property is a necessity in order to prevent paying too much for the property. The fair market price for an investment property can be found from a comparable market analysis, or CMA. Another method for determining the fair market value of an investment property is through a method known as the "capitalization rate", or Cap Rate for short. The Cap Rate of a rental property is found by taking its net operating income, or NOI, and dividing it by the property's market

value. This ratio, expressed as a percentage, should be equal to (or greater) than the average cap rates of similar investment properties in the area. For the rental property purchase, the financing method and costs should be investigated and determined prior to making an offer on the property. In this manner, it is also wise to get pre-approved for financing at a lending institution. Getting pre-approved for a mortgage definitely provides a buyer with more credibility, clout and leverage in the marketplace with the seller.

4.   Property Management - To manage or not to manage, that is the question you must ask yourself. This is because once you purchase a rental property, you'll have the choice of either managing the property yourself as a diy landlord, or you can outsource the day-to-day property management tasks to a real estate property management firm. Factors that can influence your decision are the size of the property, the amount of personal time that you can dedicate to managing the property, your property management knowledge and skills, and your temperament for the job. If you find that managing the property yourself "is not your cup of tea", then hiring a property management firm is your alternative. Property management firms typically charge a percentage of the rents collected as their management fee. But beware - not all property management firms are

created equal. There are plenty of unethical firms in the property management business. They'll be glad to place a poorly screened tenant into your vacant apartment, just to collect a quick "one month's rent" commission for filling the vacancy. Then shortly thereafter, all sorts of problems with the tenant begin, disrupting your rental operation until the tenant is evicted. So, if you choose to hire an outside management firm, exercise caution and investigate their credentials and client track record thoroughly before hiring them. The time you spend checking their history could save you plenty of grief and money in the future.

5.   Rental Income of the Property - In an attempt to inflate a property's sales price, an unethical seller can falsely overstate the rental income that is actually produced by the property. To prevent this and verify actual rent levels, it is best to mail "estoppel letters" to all existing tenants occupying the property. The tenants will then have to respond by providing written confirmation of their actual rent levels charged as well as other facts about their rental or lease agreements. These could include security deposit amounts that will have to be transferred to the buyer by the seller upon sale of the property.

6.) Operating and Utility Costs - The operating, or carrying costs of a rental property directly affect its cash flow on a "dollar-for-dollar" basis. Simply stated, a cost reduction of one-dollar for an investment property results in an increased cash flow of that same dollar for the property. Since operating costs have a direct influence on a property's cash flow, it is critical for an investor to verify all such information supplied by a seller before purchasing his or her property. Unethical sellers may understate their property's actual operating costs in an attempt to inflate its sales price.

If the tenants occupying the property pay their own utility costs, it is wise to get an idea of what those costs are. When these bills are combined with the tenants rent, the result can determine the overall "affordability" of the property that is based on the average incomes of renters in the area. Utility costs that are too high can result in high tenant turnover. This may justify lower rent levels for the property.

7.) Handling Vacancies - A proper plan (or protocol) for filling vacant apartments can really lower vacancy rates for the rental property and improve its cash flow. If the rental property is located on a highly traveled road and gets lots of exposure, then a simple "for rent" sign may be all that's needed to attract plenty of potential renters. On the other hand, if the property is somewhat secluded, then a plan for media advertising will be needed to announce the vacancy and attract qualified renters.

8.) Distance Factor of the Property - If you're an "absentee landlord", the distance of the rental property from your home can become an important factor if you plan on managing the property yourself. If the property is located quite a distance away, it may become a chore in itself just to get to the property to address tenant issues, perform maintenance, etc.

On the other hand, a rental property that is located within a convenient distance from your residence will make it easier and less time consuming for you to get to the property and carry out your on-site tasks. Over time, this can result in better (and more reliable) management and upkeep of the rental property.

9.) Parking / Laundry facilities - Adequate on-site parking facilities can be a significant benefit for tenants occupying the property. The property should have a sufficient number of parking spaces for the tenants in order to provide convenience and safety of their vehicles. If parking is not sufficient, then it's a sure bet that problems will develop with the tenants over the situation, leading to turnover and lost income.

Another significant benefit for tenants is a rental property that has adequate on-site laundry facilities. Tenants will certainly appreciate the convenience of it versus having to lug their laundry to a laundromat each week. Also, a coin-operated laundry facility can provide an additional source of income for the property owner.

10.) Investment Goals and Planning - The importance of this aspect of rental property investing could rank it at the top of the list. Simply investing in rental property alone is not enough to achieve your full potential as an investor - it only forms part of the process. To realize your full potential as an investor, you must first establish a set of goals you'd like to achieve. Then a realistic investment plan will have to be developed that will allow you to reach those goals. Such a plan can act as your "blueprint" to investment success.

These are the core issues that should be contemplated before investing your hard-earned money in rental property. Taking the time to do so and adopting this "look before you leap" mentality can certainly increase your level of investment success.

CHAPTER 10
GETTING STARTED IN REAL ESTATE WITH LITTLE OR NO MONEY

H ere are some strategies for financially-constrained aspiring investors to begin generating real estate cash flow.

You Don't Have to Own a Property to Make Money From It - Be a Dealer

There are two types of quick-sale real estate investors - retailers and dealers. Retailers buy properties outright and sell them for a quick profit. Their risk is highest, but so is their potential reward. Contrary to the late-night realty televangelists, retailers typically need substantial cash for a down payment, and at least decent credit.

Dealers, by contrast, buy and sell contracts, not properties. They find bargain properties and sign purchase contracts with their sellers. Dealers then sell these purchase contracts to retailers, making a solid profit in the process. This is known as "assignment of contract." Usually, the only cash required is the earnest money to secure the deal. A good dealer can then flip the contract for a quick $1,000 to $3,000 without ever taking possession of the deed.

Use a Double Closing for Greater Profit Potential

A double closing allows a dealer to earn a higher profit margin than an assignment of contract. With an assignment of contract, there is always potential that the deal will ultimately fall through. The dealer is protected in this case because she has already received her proceeds from the sale of the contract, but the retailer who buys the contract from her is wary of the deal falling through, and thus, will factor it into the price he is willing to pay. With a double closing, the dealer assumes more risk, because if the deal falls through, she receives nothing. However, with this greater risk comes a greater reward.

A double closing begins with the dealer signing a purchase contract with the property owner. Then the dealer signs a contract with the retailer, in which the retailer agrees to buy the property from the dealer at a higher price, and deposits that amount in escrow. The property owner signs the deed to the dealer, who then signs it to the retailer. The retailer then signs the loan documents, and the process is complete - the property owner is paid his asking price, and the dealer is paid the difference. Note that the dealer came to the table with no money, and her credit was never an issue.

Be a Scout - No Cash or Credit Required

In addition to dealers and retailers, scouts are a third type of real estate "flipper." Instead of flipping actual properties or contracts, scouts flip information.

Scouts face even less risk than dealers, and have almost no cash or credit concerns. They simply gather information about distressed properties and sell it to interested dealers and retailers. In effect, scouts do the dirty work for real estate investors, and investors are willing to pay them handsomely for doing it. Typically a scout will gather the following data on a potential deal: The owner's name and contact information, the asking price, information about the mortgage and whether payments are current, outstanding liens on the property, a photograph of the house, and pertinent information about the owner's motivation to sell - i.e. is he in the middle of a divorce, foreclosure, job transfer, etc.

Investors typically pay scouts between $500 and $1,000 for good information, but what happens if an investor doesn't pay? Simple - don't take any more deals to them. Successful investors realize the value of good information, and they are more than willing to pay for it.

Take Over the Seller's Mortgage Payments

Prior to 1989, almost all home loans were freely assumable. This meant that anyone could take over the payment of the loans without objection from the lender. However, due to a climate of rising interest rates that began in the late eighties, virtually all home loans issued since then contain a "due-on-sale" clause. This means that when ownership of a property is transferred, the lender can demand payment, in-full, of the outstanding loan.

However, "due-on-sale" is merely a clause - not a law. It is the lender's prerogative as to whether or not this clause is exercised. If you buy a property and take over the loan payments, there is a distinct possibility that the lender won't even notice. There's an even greater chance that the lender will choose not to exercise the due-on-sale clause, so long as you make timely payments. After all, the cost of enforcing the clause is significant, and as long as the lender is being paid, it is unlikely to care who signs the monthly checks. Armed with this knowledge, you can potentially buy properties without a credit check.

Real Estate Success Always Requires an Investment

There are ways to profit from real estate without significant financial investment, however, that is not to say that success comes free and easy. At the very least, you will need to make a substantial investment in yourself. In order to succeed, you must be willing to work hard. Even with a million dollar real estate portfolio, your brain will always be your #1 asset. Be sure to invest in your education on a daily basis, and learn as much as possible about your local market, real estate law, and investment strategies.

CHAPTER 11
HOW CAN AN INVESTMENT IN RENTAL PROPERTY PAY OFF REALLY WELL?

As you more than likely already know, investment in rental property can be extremely lucrative. However, while many people don't really know enough about it in order to use it to their advantage, many others will still attempt to become involved, only to discover that they end up losing a huge amount of money. Obviously, when this happens it can be soul destroying and that is why it is so important for you to educate yourself accordingly, before you actually become involved. Providing you do, you'll be able to ensure that your investment in rental property is as lucrative for you as it is for so many others.

First of all a little bit of time and energy has to be spent in researching out the right investment, which is going to give you the best returns in the future. You can either look into the option of buying just one family home or perhaps you would like to invest your money in apartment complexes. Many people go in for an eclectic mixture of both types of properties. Nevertheless it is always a very sensible idea to start off with just a limited number of properties. You can expand your business as soon as you get to know more about investing in rental property, in a slow and steady manner.

Speaking in general terms, you have two options in which you can invest in the rental property business. You can either buy a property from a seller by paying the market-rate of the property that is being sold. On the other hand, you could go to different county tax sales where plenty of properties are available at a fraction of their market price. Of course, most times you will have to expend some money in the renovation of these properties in order to obtain a handsome profit at the end of the day. But these are places where you can get good bargains at a fraction of the real market price.

After the property has been bought, one needs to check with the administration to see if any special licenses, as well as permits need to be taken out before the property is rented out. If one fails to get these permits and other legal documents, he might not make an expected profit out of his investment.

Once you've taken care of all the legal technicalities, then you can go ahead and begin renting your property, but obviously you to will need to take certain precautions in terms of who you rent it out to. Of course, for legal reasons, you're not permitted to discriminate, but you can however still make sure that you're renting it out to a tenant that can be relied on to pay the rent on time each month. One of the best ways to ensure that you rent your property to a decent tenant is to run a credit check and a background check on them beforehand. Alternatively, you could also ask them to provide you with references from past landlords.

A lease agreement needs to be signed irrespective of whether you are renting out the property for a month or for an unspecific period of time. A signed contract is going to have every single point laid out clearly like when is the rent due, what are the grounds for evicting the tenants, as well as outlining the property's condition when the tenants moved in.

It is a legal lease agreement and contract that allows you to qualify for landlord insurance policies. These policies can protect you against incurred losses due to property damage or if your tenant defaults on the payment of the rent. This insurance policy is going to ensure that your investment in rental property is secure and safe.

One knows that one needs to do a large number of things to make sure that his investment turns out to be a lucrative proposition. But all of these things need to be done as a part and parcel of being a land lord. Many people get disappointed when they do not begin to see immediate profits on their investment. After all, they have put in a large amount of money in just acquiring that property. But the main point is, patience is going to play out in the long run and you are going to make a profit on your investment in rental property.

CHAPTER 12
ARE RENTALS THE WAY TO
MAKE MONEY?

An investment in rental property can be a good way to make passive income. Make sure you go into this venture well informed. It's not enough to just buy a property and think people are going to automatically be knocking at the door to rent it. You have to understand the rental property market in the area, the attitude of prospective tenants and the condition of the property for rent. Being a landlord is hard work. If you're up for it, it can be very rewarding.

Making an investment in rental property is not the same situation as buying your primary residence. You may think about different qualities when considering a rental property. Are you looking for a property that will be for a family or for several different tenants? What type of tenants do you want to have in your property? If you buy rental property near a college town you might get plenty of tenants but they may not be as long term as a family in a different community. You also need to consider how much rent the market will bear. If you make an investment in a rental property and can't get enough rent to make a profit, you may regret it.

A successful investment in rental property means keeping your property rented. You have to actively seek tenants and then you must do whatever it takes to keep those tenants happy. This means maintaining the property, making repairs quickly, and responding to your tenants when they need something.

Sometimes it's easier to have a property management firm take the responsibility of managing the rental property if you are not close enough or do not have the time. This will eat away at some of your investment profit but in the long run it may be worth it. Property management companies can perform all the tasks associated with the rental property investment such as recruiting and screening tenants, collecting rent, and managing repairs. For many people, the fee is well worth it.

CHAPTER 13
TIPS FOR INVESTING IN RENTAL PROPERTIES

Are you considering investing in rental properties? For a beginner, investing in rental properties may seem like a daunting task. However, with these 5 simple tips, you'll be on your way in no time!

Tip 1: Put Yourself in the Right Frame of Mind

What does putting yourself in the right frame of mind mean? First, realize that investing in rental properties is business. You must put aside the conceptions that an investment property must be beautiful, have excellent curb appeal, exciting amenities and a wonderful floor plan. A beginner may lose money or miss out on making real money because the income property doesn't have those things.

You must believe that beauty is only skin deep and instead look at the property's financial performance.

Tip 2: Set Meaningful Goals

Just by answering these few questions, you can set realistic and meaningful goals that will help you successfully invest in rental properties.

- Do you have the available funds to realistically invest in an income property?

- Do you expect a return on investment immediately?

- Are you expecting your return on investment when you resell?

- Do you plan to keep the property long term, or do you plan on reselling right away?

- How much of your own time, effort and money can you afford to contribute to running the property?

Tip 3: Do Market Research

As a beginner in investing in rental properties, you probably don't know much about the prices for rentals in your local market. Before actually investing in a property, take some time to learn as much as you can about local income property values, rent rates and occupancy rates. The more you know, the better equipped you are to see a property for what it is: a good deal or a bad one. The following resources will get you on your way.

- A local appraiser

- The county tax assessor

- A qualified real estate agent

- A local property management company

Tip 4: Learn How to Run Your Own Numbers

There are several key financial measures that are used to evaluate a property. Once you know what income, expenses, cash flow and rate of return are, you will be in a better position to make good investment decisions.

There are several software programs for this specific purpose. Find one that's right for you and you'll be amazed how much you can learn by running your own numbers and viewing the reports.

Tip 5: Only Work with a Licensed Real Estate Agent

Once you're ready to start investing in rental properties, contact a local, licensed real estate agent. Your agent can inform you of local market conditions and recommend properties that meet your particular investing goals.

Make it clear to your agent that you want to invest in

rental properties. Your agent should be able to present you with concise data to make smart investment decisions.

CHAPTER 14
USING YOUR RETIREMENT FUNDS TO INVEST IN RENTAL PROPERTY

S hould you use your retirement funds to invest in rental property? The stock market may go through a long period of wild swings and at the same time real estate prices have dropped dramatically in many areas.

Two tsunami's have swamped the financial world in past years,and these events provide a great opportunity. The stock market is down by 50% since its peak in 2007 and you are wondering how you are going to retire or what to do with your investments. At the same time housing prices have collapsed in many areas while interest rates are at all time lows.

If you are like most people you are afraid for the future and uncertain about what to do. But to those who have some vision, now may be a time to take advantage of a golden opportunity. It is a great time to take advantage of low real estate prices. In many areas mortgage payments (PITI) are lower than rents. Real estate prices are cyclical in nature and will increase again despite what the pessimists say. So why not take advantage of low prices and invest in rental property?

You may be thinking that you don't have the money but if you have a retirement account there could be a solution to your dilemma about what to do with your retirement accounts. Why not borrow against your 401k or use a self-directed IRA to fund a real estate purchase?

In general it is not a good idea to borrow against your 401k (to buy a car or fund a vacation for example) but I believe it is an ideal vehicle to use for real estate investments. I have used mine to buy 2 houses. You can borrow up to $50,000 against your 401k and typically have multiple loans. If the loan is for your personal residence it can be a 10 year term, otherwise it can only be a 5 year term.

In a like manner, you can convert your IRA into a self-directed IRA and invest in rental property directly. All of the rental profits go directly back to your IRA and when you sell the property the profit would go to your IRA. If it is a Roth IRA all of that profit is not taxed!

Maybe your don't have an IRA. I'll bet someone you know does and would be interested in earning a steady income from loaning you money from their IRA. Just develop a business plan and sell the idea to them. These are just a couple of ideas for using your retirement funds to invest in rental property.

CHAPTER 15
DISCOVER THE TRUTH
ABOUT MAKING MONEY

aking money is really not a hard thing to do once you know how to do it, but it is the researches and tests and trials that probably put most of you down. You need to discover the truth about making money first before you can start making money without having any big problems. You need to realize this one simple fact, and you will be able to make money out of anything you do. That small single fact is that making money is not an easy thing to do in the first place.

A lot of people make the mistake of concluding that making money can be an easy job to do. Well, it is kind of hard to disappoint you but, they are not. There are a lot of efforts, energy, time, and money spent in the entire moneymaking process; it is the true nature of businesses. This single fact is what successful believe in. That is why it is not hard for them to make more money, making them rich in what seems to be an easy process.

They still invest their money, spend their time managing the business and money flow, do all the required efforts and then do some more, and of course learn from their failures. You will, eventually, discover how to make the entire process a bit easier. It will not change the fact that making money is not an easy process. It is not something you will get for granted, and you will never be able to get it at all if you are not believing this. You will also be able to learn from your mistakes, doing it better and better each time you try it. That is why making money looks like an easy thing to do.

As you can see, coming to a point where you realize that making money needs a lot of hard work, there is no way you can make money doing nothing. You have to put some, if not all, of your efforts, time, and energies to actually make money. Believe me when I say that it will be worth all the sacrifices. All that you put into your moneymaking process will trade off and get you there. Now that you know the truth about making money, all you have to do now is go out there and do your best.

THE TRUTH ABOUT "EASY MONEY"

In your quest for easy money, have you asked yourself just how easy you are hoping or expecting the money to come to you? The word "easy" is a comparative term. It has no meaning until you answer the question, "easy compared to what?"

Some people, who want easy money, want to receive

it as a gift or handout - without any work or effort on their part. I'm sure you have met such people. They seem to think the world owes them something. Short of a year or two of intensive psychotherapy, there isn't much that can really help these folks. Their lifelong quest for easy money is doomed from the outset. To these folks I can only say: "look for a good therapist" - preferably one that excels at Bioenergetics, NLP, and Ericksonian Hypnosis.

So, I'll assume you are willing to make some effort on your own financial behalf - and further, that you are not in desperate straits, financially or emotionally. When you are desperate, nothing is easy. For you to implement the suggestions that I am going to share with you will require some patience on your part. Money comes to you much more easily when you don't try to "push the river" - rivers flow just fine when you are able to do the requisite work as if you had all the time in the world - even when you don't.

Financially, there are many accomplishments that are very difficult under some circumstances. For instance, it is next to impossible to become financially independent by working for someone else. Still it can be done while also holding down a job - though it takes quite a bit of discipline to do so. For some the dislike of their job is a great motivator.

Returning to the question of how "easy" is easy:

o It is easier to succeed with relevant skills than without - but skills can be learned. Are you willing to apply yourself to the learning?

o It is easier to succeed if you already have money that you can afford to invest than if you don't. In the absence of such capital you will need to invest more time. Are you willing to do this?

o It is vastly easier to succeed if you are willing to learn from the mistakes of others - otherwise you will have to make a lot of expensive and time-consuming mistakes on your own. My website is a great place to avoid that particular pitfall - but, again, you will need to take the time to study the lessons contained in it. Will you do so?

In your quest for "easy money" - or even just "easier money", which is far more achievable, you will need to understand the distinction between earning money and making money.

CHAPTER 16
LEARN THE TRUTH ABOUT MAKING MONEY IN THIS ECONOMY

When life knocks us down we can feel so hopeless we hide in bed under the covers. Breathing is difficult under those covers, is it not? At some point we have to crawl out of the armor of our cocoon we found so comforting and start over.

Let me share with you a practical live story

Her cost was fifteen dollars resulting in thirteen calls. Cassie typed out a simple agreement to clean a customer's house once a week for a year. She prepared a questionnaire which she used during the interviews, asking about special needs including birthdays and anniversaries. As her customers signed their contracts, Cassie requested three months advance pay, plus monthly payments. She quickly reached her limit of twenty customers a month by giving good service and receiving referrals.

But she went the extra mile. Prior to leaving each home clean and smelling fresh, she placed a rose and a candy mint on the bedroom pillows. Each evening before bedtime, she prepared hand-written thank you notes for first time customers, and always sent birthday, or holiday cards for the families.

Cassie built a solid lucrative business with nothing but hope. Living within her means by saving and investing wisely, she helped her children graduate college. Today with her children being successful and her investments safe, she travels two months each year, and has paid off her home loan as well as secured a good retirement income.

Making money is not rocket science. It's about the knowledge, skill, or talents we have and then sharing with people who can benefit. In return money moves in life and when people see their money moving needs are met and opportunities appear.

Gratitude builds hope and eliminates fear. When fear is conquered people can move forward just as Cassie did. Abraham Lincoln and Rosa Parks are wonderful examples for us to follow. Fear and hopelessness couldn't stop these two great people. Is is going to stop you?

You are unique. Your identity is who your are, not your life status. Knowledge from life experiences can help other people, and begin moving money for your needs and opportunities. Take the step, it's worth the effort.

There are many reasons for unemployment, loss of job, no jobs available, loss of business, recession, even health problems, are just a few. With a little hope a new start is certain if the first step is taken with gratitude. Life experiences can close one door but open double doors to opportunity.

Cassie quit school and married at a young age. Her husband a successful business owner convinced her to stay home and focus on being a wife and mother. Had Cassie known that her husband would leave her with two children to raise and no education six years she no doubt would have made a different choice.

Being alone and frightened Cassie went to bed and hid under the covers for a few weeks. Knowing her children needed her, with fear and limited hope she crawled out of bed to start a new life. She listed her skills and talents on paper. While writing she realized she could easily build relationships with strangers, and clean a house until it sparkled. She created her plan of action with prayer and hope, and placed an ad in a local newspaper.

Her cost was fifteen dollars resulting in thirteen calls. Cassie typed out a simple agreement to clean a customer's house once a week for a year. She prepared a questionnaire which she used during the interviews, asking about special needs including birthdays and anniversaries. As her customers signed their contracts, Cassie requested three months advance pay, plus monthly payments. She quickly reached her limit of twenty customers a month by giving good service and receiving referrals.

But she went the extra mile. Prior to leaving each home clean and smelling fresh, she placed a rose and a candy mint on the bedroom pillows. Each evening before bedtime, she prepared hand-written thank you notes for first time customers, and always sent birthday, or holiday cards for the families.

Cassie built a solid lucrative business with nothing but hope. Living within her means by saving and investing wisely, she helped her children graduate college. Today with her children being successful and her investments safe, she travels two months each year, and has paid off her home loan as well as secured a good retirement income.

Making money is not rocket science. It's about the knowledge, skill, or talents we have and then sharing with people who can benefit. In return money moves in life and when people see their money moving needs are met and opportunities appear.

Gratitude builds hope and eliminates fear. When fear

is conquered people can move forward just as Cassie did. Abraham Lincoln and Rosa Parks are wonderful examples for us to follow. Fear and hopelessness couldn't stop these two great people. Is is going to stop you?

You are unique. Your identity is who your are, not your life status. Knowledge from life experiences can help other people, and begin moving money for your needs and opportunities. Take the step, it's worth the effort.

There are many reasons for unemployment, loss of job, no jobs available, loss of business, recession, even health problems, are just a few. With a little hope a new start is certain if the first step is taken with gratitude. Life experiences can close one door but open double doors to opportunity.

CHAPTER 17
CAN INVESTMENT IN RENTAL PROPERTY MAKE YOU RICH?

With all the hype about rising property prices today, rental properties have become the preferred choice for both locals and expatriates. As a result, many may wonder, "Can investment in rental property make you rich?"

Well, yes you can be rich and successful IF you know how to make your investment work for you. Investing in rental properties have become an excellent option for serious investors who wish to leverage on these properties, get maximum tax deductions from them as well as secure equity gains to ensure a steady flow of income each month.

Indeed, this requires a whole lot of business strategy and planning.

Being a landlord provides you with an alternate source of income on top of your existing job or similar investments. However, you should be aware that renting a property is way more complex and has many risks and advantages that come along with it. In other words, it is more than just acquiring a property, renting it out and kicking back to relax while waiting for the cash to roll in.

As an investor, you need to look into the nitty gritty details of managing a property. You need to know about the neighborhood that your property is in, its living conditions and the demographics of the people living in the area. Doing so will help ensure that your money is invested in the right location and property. In addition, you should be aware of the laws and regulations that all property owners and tenants have to abide by. Also, you need to ensure that you have a good long-term investment plan to maximize your earnings. Moreover, you ought to hire a real estate attorney to ensure that all your legal matters are well taken care of. Getting one will be a good investment, as he or she will help keep your legal works in order.

Besides, you should always obtain as much information about potential or existing tenants of the rented property if possible. Information regarding their rental agreements or ability to fulfill lease requirements will give you a heads up when looking for or securing a good tenant for your property.

An investment will not be successful if you have a property that is left vacant and unattended to. As such, you need to ensure that you are constantly seeking out new tenants, even if it means putting up advertisements in the papers or online property listings. Furthermore, ensuring that the property you are renting out is in tiptop condition helps to make your property more appealing to potential tenants.

Fortunately for property investors, there has been an increase in the number of people seeking properties to rent. This is especially so since property prices have been rising, divorce rates are gradually increasing and more and more people are finding it hard to keep their jobs today. This has resulted in both young and old switching to renting instead of buying homes. As such, taking the necessary steps and strategizing for a good long-term investment plan will allow you to take advantage of this market.

CHAPTER 18
TIPS FOR INVESTING IN RENTAL PROPERTIES - TIPS TO BECOME SUCCESSFUL

Whether you want to invest in real estate as a full time job or just make some extra money, don't be afraid of the current state of economic affairs. Investing in real estate has and will always be a great way to make money. Here are some tips for investing in rental property.

When it comes to the type of property you purchase, of course you want to look for a good value. Lately there are tons of houses available through auction or foreclosure. You can also find many deals that are in pre-foreclosure. Look around in the neighborhood that you are interested in. You might find some good deals without doing a lot of online searching.

Look for motivated buyers. When investing in rental property you want to get the best deal possible and you're more likely to get a better deal when the sellers want to close quickly and move on. Some motivated buyers are:

1. people who have already bought their next house.

Right now they are paying two mortgages. Or sometimes they can't close on their new deal until they have sold the old house.

2. a couple who is going through a divorce. Most will try to sell the joint property to make a clean break.

3. a landlord who is unhappy with current tenants or unable to handle the responsibility of rental properties. Some people may start out in real estate thinking it's a good business idea, but just don't have what it takes to be successful.

4. an out of town property owner. It can be very hard to manage a property when you're not close by to make inspections or arrange for maintenance. This owner may be looking to unload the out of town property and find something closer to home.

Another tip for investing in rental property successfully is to find property in a good location. You can get top rental dollar for a place that is close to popular amenities such as public transportation and eating places. If you're targeting college students with no cars you want to find a place within walking distance of the things they need to get to. Figure out who you want to market to and think about the things that they will want.

CHATPER 19
WHY YOU NEED LEASES WHEN INVESTING IN RENTAL PROPERTY

When you are investing in rental property, you need to understand both landlord and tenant rights. Often times, landlord-tenant relations are not regulated by any state agency. State statutes are what define landlord and tenant rights. The rights of each party should be listed is a lease agreement. Below are some of the items that need to be included in a lease.

Security Deposit and Rent Amount

In every state, the security deposit cannot exceed a certain amount of monthly rent. Once you are investing in rental property and find renters, there needs to be an agreement of the amount and when it is due. Included in this agreement is what happens if rent is late. It is illegal for a landlord to take tenants' property for unpaid rent.

Lease Time

There needs to be a specific time listed of how long the renters plan to stay. You need this in case the tenant needs to leave before the lease time is up. Usually, there is some sort of financial penalty if the tenant decides to break the lease early. When investing in rental property, you need time to find a new tenant as soon as possible. It is standard practice that tenants must give 30-days notice before moving out. Make sure you include this in the lease to keep surprises to a minimum.

Pets

You need to discuss your policy about pets with tenants and include it in the lease. Whether you decide to allow pets or not is a personal preference.

Inspection Rights

You need to protect your investment when you are investing in rental property. Conducting periodic inspections will help you do that. You need to decide how often you would like to inspect the property for damages. You should also layout the inspection procedures for tenants, so they are not taken off guard.

Payments for Utilities

As a landlord, you will need to decide how the utilities will be paid. Utilities can be part of the rent that tenants pay. You can also waive some or all of the utility costs. Deciding who will pay for the utilities will be up to you.

Having a written lease protects you as you are investing in rental property. Make sure to discuss all items of a lease with the tenants before you both sign it. Without a written agreement, you are leaving yourself open to a wide variety of problems.

CHAPTER 20
THE TRUTH ABOUT HARD
MONEY LENDERS

So many first time investors are curious about hard money lenders. Who are they? What is it? How do I get some? Is it beneficial? Let me share with you some of the basic principals about hard money lenders. First of all, lets determine what the term "hard money" means. When money is discussed between investors, it is considered to either be "soft" or "hard". Typically soft money is easier to qualify for and the terms are flexible. Hard money, on the other hand, is just the opposite.It is much more restrictive. Not in that it's more difficult to obtain, but the terms are very specific and much more strict. They have to be, because most hard money comes from private individuals with a great deal of money on hand. This is why hard money is also referred to as "private money". The money used for investment purposes comes from people, just like you and I, not a typical lending institution. So their first priority is to protect their investment capital. This is why the terms have to be so strict. If it were your money, you would want the same.

So what are some of the terms of "hard money lenders"? Obviously it

varies from lender to lender. It used to be that hard money lenders would lend

solely based upon the deal or property at hand. They would only lend up to a

certain percentage of the fair market value of the property, that way in the event of

default, the hard money lender would profit handsomely if they had to foreclose or

sell to an end buyer. Now, you will find that many hard money lenders, if they want

to stay in business, require more than just equity to qualify. This is because the

laws now are favorable for consumers. Consumer protection laws, time consuming

and expensive court procedures, and so on have forced some hard money lenders

to become even harsher when applying for a loan.

It is good to know what the terms are when dealing with a hard money

lender so you can find the one that will fit your needs. Here are some of the terms you can expect to see. Typically they will only loan you up to 70% ARV (after

repaired value). This means that a hard money lender can loan you up to

70% of what the home is worth in repaired condition. So if you find a home worth

$45,000 in the condition it's in, and needs $20,000 in repair work, and after it is

repaired the current fair market value is worth $100,000, then typically they can

lend you up to $70,000, which would cover the cost of the house and the repairs.

Other terms you can expect are high interest rates. Interest rates vary from 12% -

20% annually and terms can last for 6 months to a few years. Many times these

rates vary depending on your credit score and experience. In most cases, there will

be closing costs or fees to use hard money. Typically hard money lenders will

charge anywhere from 2-10 points. One point equals one percent of the mortgage

amount. So charging 1 point on a $100,000 loan would

be $1000. These are all

important things to consider when choosing a hard money lender.

Other things to consider are how quickly funds will be available. Many times, when

you find investment properties, you need to move quickly. Your ability to get access

to money quickly can make all the difference. It's important to begin relationships

with potential hard money lenders as quickly as possible. You also need to be

aware of pre-payment penalties. Pre-payment penalties can really hurt your deal

and cut into your profits substantially. Try to avoid pre-payment penalties.

Many hard money lenders today will also require you to fill out a credit

application that may ask you for W-2's and or tax returns, your most recent pay

stubs, and bank statements. Again, it's all about protecting their assets. Yet, some

like the old fashion way where they only care about the deal so they do a drive by or physically look at the property. Again it all depends on whom you deal with.

When should you use a hard money lender? Hard money is great for

beginning investors who may not have money or for those who have bad credit and

cannot qualify. Investors also use hard money when they need to purchase quickly.

Typical soft money or conventional loans take 30 days or more. Sometimes that is

to long. Using a hard money lender is also a creative way to finance a property.

Most like to call it "Nothing Down". If you can borrow enough money to buy the

property, fix it up and then sell it under market value for a profit, then you've just

made money without any of your own money. Sure it will cost you money to borrow

that money, but the rewards out way the expense.

How can you find hard money lenders? There are hundreds of hard

money lenders waiting to lend you money. It could be your next door neighbor.

The best way to find hard money lenders is to talk to a mortgage company and ask

for referrals. You can also call a title company or a real estate agency. They deal

with buyers and sellers of houses every day. Shop around until you find the best

one that will fit your needs. Another way is search online for hard money lenders.

Some will lend nationwide - these typically want a credit check. If you find a hard

money lender in your area, they may just do a drive by.

CHAPTER 21
INVESTMENT IN RENTAL PROPERTIES - HOW TO BUY RENTAL PROPERTIES

Many financially savvy people make investments in rental properties. How to buy rental properties is the focus of this article. The traditional way to buy properties has been to apply for bank loans and pay a 20% down payment to secure the loan. At the height of our real estate and credit bubble, national mortgage companies were approving no money down loans with 100% financing. We all know now that this turned out to be a bad idea.

Today we have an investment environment where banks don't want to make loans, and people don't want to risk losing any of their capital. Sellers are not selling many properties and the prices have come way down. This makes it a great time to invest in rental properties if you can pull off the purchase. Here are some ways that may help you to buy rental properties.

First you should check your credit and start to repair it if necessary. See if a bank will prequalify you for a mortgage loan, which would provide you with funds to make investments in rental properties. If your credit holds you back, you can simply find a credit partner.

Start forming banking relationships with the local banks that are currently providing local mortgages. You will need to have knowledge, income, and savings to the bank's satisfaction. If your savings or income is not sufficient, you may be able to appeal to a partner with those strengths. If your knowledge is not sufficient, invest in learning first.

If you aren't able to secure a bank loan, there are still other options such as owner financing, land contracts, and lease purchasing.

CHAPTER 22
TIPS ON INVESTING IN RENTAL PROPERTY - 5 TIPS THAT WILL MAKE OR BREAK YOUR PROPERTY BUSINESS

Anyone who is searching for tips on investing in rental property will probably have realised what a lucrative way of making money this can be. They will probably also know that many of the richest people in the World have either made their money from property or now use property as their preferred investment vehicle to build their wealth.

This chapter gives 5 top tips that will help you to realise your dreams of making money from property or propel your property business forward at an even quicker rate.

1. Buy with your head not with your heart - perhaps the biggest mistake that is made by those new to making money from property is buying with their heart and not their head. It does not matter if it is not the sort of property that you would live in or in the sort of area that you would want to bring up your kids in. What matters is the bottom

line profit. That said, you do need to make sure that the property is reasonable and that it is not in a location where the windows are going to be broken every other week. The most important thing is to make sure it is in a location that is in demand by tenants.

2. Have multiple exit strategies - whenever you buy a property you need to already know how you are going to make money. Your exit strategy would normally mean that the property you are buying is in a locating where it is easy to sell those types of properties. You will also want to make sure that you know it is able to rent well and even that your tenants might have the option to buy the property off you in the future if you choose to sell.

3. Buy at a discount - you will not get very far by buying property at the retail price. You need to buy it at its wholesale price; at a discount. This is the goal, even if you have a large amount of money to put into the property in the first place. The more profit you can lock in at the outset the better.

4. Know your strategy - you have to know what your goals are and why you are buying the particular property you are buying and why you are buying it in the particular location you are buying it. Everything else follows on from this. If you don't get your strategy right you are going to be treading water from day one.

5. Be in the game for the long term - many budding property investors make the big mistake of selling to soon because of a fear of interest rate rises, or some other impending doom to the property market. The real money in property is made when you are in it for the long run. Don't bail out to soon. Be prepared to either never sell your properties or at least hold onto them for seven years plus.

CHAPTER 23
HOW TO FIND GOOD INVESTMENT AND RENTAL PROPERTY

Real estate investors all face a very common challenge: locating appropriate and quality investment properties. While there are a ton of online real estate websites that let you search for property, there seem to be just as many real estate investment clubs that want to sell you their own holdings. How do you know what is a good deal? What should you look for in a good rental or investment property and where can you find them? Let's take a look at some basics that will be an excellent refresher for the experienced real estate investor and useful tips for the novice alike.

1. What are you buying? When you decide to purchase an investment or rental property, determine what your goals are in advance. Whether it's a buy-and-hold, short-term flip, rehab-and-rent or purely a prime rental property, you're less likely to be sidetracked by all the properties available out there. You'll also be able to develop a list of targeted questions to bring to the table on every property you're considering if you know your

investment goals specifically and in advance or purchase.

2. Who are you buying it from? When shopping for investment property, there are many investment clubs that masquerade as "clubs" just to get you to join and then sell you property exclusively owned by the club or other members. While this alone should not discount any of their holdings or member properties, you should exercise the same extensive due diligence you would if the property were not presented to you by the real estate investment club.

3. Do your research. When buying an investment or rental property, the numbers and data have to make sense. A "good price" alone is not enough to move forward with a purchase. You should research vacancy rates, average rents, annual property expenses, and have a full inspection and appraisal done on any property you're considering.

4. Cash flow - know where you're at. At the purchase price, will the income from the property on an annual basis fall below, meet or exceed its annual expenses? Are you prepared to cash flow negative if the property is vacant or expenses exceed income? If you've clearly defined your goals for the property you're looking to acquire, you'll be able to determine your cash flow needs. In many cases, your cash flow needs will dictate your

purchase goals as well!

5. P/E Ratios - do they make sense? The P/E (price-to-earning) ratio of a property is a simple equation of the property's purchase price versus earnings potential. If you're considering a property in an area where purchase prices are rapidly escalating yet rents are remaining stable, you're less likely to earn money on the property as a rental. However, if you locate a property in an area where rents remain stable and favorable in relation to the purchase price, you're generally looking at a better option as a rental property because of your ability to cash flow on it regardless of market conditions. Prices go up? Great, you make money when you sell. Prices go down and rents historically hold stable? You're still cash flowing. Your real estate agent can obtain rental data for the area of the property you're considering.

6. How will you hold the property? Decide prior to your search whether you're going to be holding the property in a business entity such as an LLC or S-corp, in your own name, in a trust or in your self-directed or real estate IRA. This will ease the closing process.

When searching for an investment property, it is often useful to use a search engine that's tailored specifically for real estate investors. InvestorLoft's PropScout Search Engine is a free online tool that allows you to search by specific investment criteria like cap rate, cash flow, cash on cash return, discount percentage, down payment and more. You have to register for their site to utilize it, but registration is free. Tools like this are useful in that the search results are highly relevant to a real estate investor's needs. The tool also eliminates hours of searching and sifting through information that is more important to primary residence buyers than in investor assessing the financial potential of a property.

The smartest way to find good investment and rental property is to begin with the list above and align yourself with a real estate professional who is experienced in working with investors. Real estate investors have specific needs and having a solid understanding of what you're looking for and questions to ask can only be enhanced by the guidance of a knowledgeable professional in the real estate industry.

CHAPTER 24
HOW TO INVEST IN RENTAL PROPERTY

Investing in rental properties has always been a popular way to make money through real estate. Having said that, it is important to add that rental property investment is a serious business, which requires complete understanding as well as dedication on the part of the investor. There are several steps that need to be followed in order to ensure that your investment is profitable.

Firstly, it is important to understand the various kinds of properties that are available for investment and narrow down on the one that appeals you the most. Properties include single family units, multifamily units, vacation homes and the like. Narrowing down your type will help you find the property that works best for you. Secondly, selecting the geographical area that you want for your rental property investment will also help you in choosing faster and making a good decision. If you are new to the field of rental properties, then enlisting the services of a realtor, especially one with a good reputation, will help you in your search.

While searching for rental properties, always look for multiple places before you finalize on one. This will help give you an idea about the various properties and the rents that are available in the area, which in turn will help you in choosing the best option, based on your requirements and needs. A realtor will help you identify the best property that suits your needs and requirements.

Once the property is identified, the next step is to find a money source or bank to help fund your purchase. Mortgages, if any, on your property will have to be taken into account while finally calculating your profits or returns from the property. Estimating the possible rental income from the property is another important step, which will help in determining your cash flow. Prospective rental incomes can be identified from classified advertisements in the newspapers for that area.

Always be prepared for various expenses like repairs, maintenance, taxes and the like, which accrue on property. Additionally, make sure that you count your mortgage payments and other charges that are classified as outgoings. The net difference between the expenses and the income will be you resultant cash flow, which can be positive or negative, depending on a variety of factors. Once the outgoings are determined in advance, it is possible to ensure that the income is higher, so that your net cash flow is positive.

Tax repercussions of rental property investment should be studied before investing in such properties. Therefore, it is always advisable to discuss property investments with your tax consultant before actually making them. Buying properties, if done through an attorney, will mean lesser problems. Similarly, finding a good tenant is the crux to making a profitable rental property investment. Therefore, interview several before finalizing one. Once the tenant is finalized, make sure that you have a proper rental agreement and make sure that both parties are aware of the various clauses.

Management of the rental property is very important. The most important factor is to understand who will manage the property. Therefore, ensure that you are clear on what aspects you will manage and what the tenant has to manage on his or her own. Similarly, if you are operating through a property management consultant, ensure that they also clear on these aspects.

CHAPTER 25
THE TRUTH ABOUT NO
MONEY DOWN REAL ESTATE
DEALS

Anyone who has ever been a victim of insomnia has probably been subjected to the late night infomercials that promise "real estate riches with no money down". An integral part of the infomercial is a series of sound-bites or testimonials from successful students telling how much real estate they bought and how quickly their lives went from rags to riches thanks to whichever fabulous course is being touted.

To be fair, you can make a lot of money in real estate and you can shorten your learning curve tremendously by buying some of these courses. You can also spend thousands of dollars and still be at a loss as to how to get started on your road to success. When you ask for help from the course sponsors, you are upsold to an expensive bootcamp or another series of DVDs and books.

Before you jump into an expensive course with both feet, take some time to investigate the courses out there and to find out exactly what is meant when someone says

"No Money Down".

No money down in almost every course I've ever subscribed to generally means "none of your money down". That's almost as good as no money down, but the money still has to come from somewhere. Some of the ways you can do a no money down deal include: 100% financing (you still pay some fees and closing costs); using other people's money (including but not limited to friends and relatives); "hard" or private money lenders; using cash advances on your credit cards; taking on a financial partner; negotiating a no money deal directly from the seller; lease option; and taking property subject to the existing loan.

The other half of the equation is the concept of "owning" or "controlling" properties. The enthusiastic and successful course alumni talk about owning a million dollars worth of real estate in a short amount of time. What they don't talk about is how much is owed on the property. If they're doing no money down deals, the amount owed is probably very close to the amount the properties are worth. Their balance sheet improves when and if the properties increase in value. For the past few years, people have made a lot of money due to the fast equity growth in many markets. Over the past six months or so, those paper profits have deflated somewhat and the equity growth has slowed considerably. Over a long period of time, equity growth is what will make people truly wealthy. But until you sell the properties or refinance and take some of the money out of the property, you are looking at paper profits. And paper profits don't put food on the table.

One of the words you will want to listen for is "cashflow". Cashflow is the amount of money the owner makes on an investment property after all the expenses are paid: mortgage, taxes, insurance, maintenance and repairs, vacancy rate, etc. A general rule of thumb is that a property will breakeven or possibly cashflow (depending on taxes, insurance, maintenance, etc.) if you can rent it for 1% of the purchase price. For example, if a three bedroom, two bath home rents for $1,200 in your area, you shouldn't pay more than $120,000 for the house, unless you want to make a substantial down payment to bring the loan amount down to $120,000. The testimonials you hear on infomercials talk about the large monthly incomes generated by real estate investments. What you don't hear is how much money goes right back out each month to cover the debt service on the properties.

Money is made in real estate when you go into the deal, not when you sell. True investors want to buy a property at the right price in order to have immediate cashflow and/or equity. Buying a property that doesn't at least break even or cashflow and hoping that the market will bring the property values up is speculating, not investing. The equity growth is the long-term payoff for an investor, not a quick money strategy.

One of the complaints I've heard about one of the more famous late night gurus is that his strategies are so old that most are no longer legal. I have his course. Some of the techniques can no longer be used. But he has a lot of other good general information in his course. With experience, you can look at some of the old, now illegal strategies and apply them to the new market and new laws.

There are all sorts of ways to do no money down deals. Whether a strategy is a new twist or an old workhorse, legality varies state to state. I recently read of a young investor who was eager to find "subject to" deals to flip to other investors or end users. "Subject to" means taking title to someone's house and keeping the loan in their name. It can trigger the "Due on Sale" clause which is included in just about every loan that is made in the U.S. The seller runs the risk that the investor or the person the investor sells the deal to will not make the payments in a timely fashion or at all and ruin the seller's credit. The young investor had bought a late night course and was eager to hit the ground running. He hasn't stopped to find out the pitfalls of that type of deal; he doesn't have the financial depth to cover the payments on the properties that he takes subject to, he will be committing loan fraud and will probably end up getting sued by a seller who will come back at him either for not making payments or for coercing him to sign over his house when he was in financial distress.

The courses you buy, the books you read, the seminars you go to are all just starting points. Each course gives another layer of knowledge and fills in gaps left by the previous courses. But you need to supplement the courses with real-world experience. One way to do that is to join a real estate investor group. Meeting with other investors will help you learn your local market, find out about other meetings and seminars and discover who is respected in the industry and who is not. If there are no groups in your area, try to go to a real estate seminar (they are usually two or three day events and range in price from $300 to $5,000 - hit the more inexpensive ones first) and meet other investors from around the country.

In most major cities, seminar companies sponsor "free" real estate seminars about every other month. The seminar usually lasts a couple of hours and it is a come-on to buy a course.

No course is any good unless you take off the shrink-wrap and use it! So many people make an impulse purchase of a course and never even open up the package. Then they'll complain that the course was no good or didn't work. Courses and seminars don't work. You have to do the work.

Investing in real estate with little or no money down is done every day. But you increase your odds of success by first educating yourself on various techniques and lowering your expectations to realistic levels. As you start reading up on real estate, work out a plan for your real estate business. Do you want to buy and hold properties? How many do you want to hold or manage? Do you want to flip properties to someone else for a fee? Do you want to use banks, hard money lenders, lease options or whatever to acquire properties? Find the techniques you are comfortable using, get your paperwork in order and learn your local marketplace before going out and buying everything in sight. There's no sense accumulating a real estate empire if you can't hold on to it. Here's one thing that is hardly ever mentioned in those late night infomercials: Do Your Homework. Real estate investing takes knowledge, experience and hard work. The courses that are out there are merely the tools you can use to make the work easier.

CHAPTER 26
REAL ESTATE INVESTING GUIDE - NO MONEY DOWN INVESTING TECHNIQUES

Many investors have come to believe that their chances of doing a $0 down real estate investing deal are about the same as catching a glimpse of bigfoot in the backyard pool. Many of the old $0 down investing methods have gone the way of the dinosaur, but some incredible new $0 down investing methods are now available. In this chapter, we are going to focus on just one of the awesome new no money down investing techniques.

One of the best no money down investing methods that I have come across is real estate wholesaling. Because wholesaling involves selling contracts like most investors sell homes it creates the perfect opportunity for the cash strapped investor. The idea of selling contracts may seem complicated initially but nothing could be farther from the truth.

Selling a contract simply involves finding a pieced of real estate that can be bought undervalue. Then writing up a real estate contract just as you would on any other home. The main difference is that instead of putting just your name on the bottom line you put your name "and/or assignees". Then whoever decides to buy the contract from you becomes the assignee. Typical profits from doing wholesaling deals are between $5,000 and $20,000.

The best part is when you have no money invested in a particular deal, even making a dollar gives you better than a 1000% return on your money. If you are a cash strapped or credit bruised buyer you may want to give real estate wholesaling a try.

CHAPTER 27
THE TRUTH ABOUT FEDERAL INCOME TAX LAWS AND SELLING YOUR HOME

Some angry e-mails have been circulating about real estate tax stating that all sales of real estate are subject to a 3.8 percent sales tax. The e-mails cite specific examples, saying that if you sell your home for $400,000, you will be subject to a $15,200 tax. Before you get mad, get the truth about federal income tax laws on capital gains relating to the sale of your house.

The e-mail is referring to a Medicare tax of 3.8% on investment or unearned income for high income taxpayers, or those individual taxpayers who report income over $200,000 and married taxpayers filing jointly who report income over $250,000. Keep in mind that in 2008, only three percent of individual taxpayers made over $200,000. Investment income is money made from investments, not including distributions from qualified retirement plans like pensions and IRAs.

Regarding selling your home, qualifying individual taxpayers can exclude up to $250,000 worth of the gain from the sale of a primary home, while qualifying married taxpayers can exclude $500,000. The e-mail is also incorrect in that this exclusion is not on the net proceeds (or how much you sell your house for), but on the gain from the sale. The taxable amount before figuring in the exclusion is calculated subtracting the basis from the sale price. The basis usually equals the original cost of your home plus capital improvements and adjustments. This gain amount is also excluded from the Medicare tax to which the e-mail refers, regardless of your income total. Consider here that the median sales price, not even the median capital gain amount, for homes in 2008 was $181,300. Taxes do apply, however, to vacation homes regardless of how much you make on the sale.

So, for the Medicare tax to actually apply to you, your income must be above the threshold amounts and your gain from the sale of your home must be above the exclusion amounts. To break this down, let's say you are single and your income is $210,000. Let's say you then sell your home which you initially bought for $400,000 for $750,000. This means that your gain from the home sale is $350,000. Since your income is over $200,000 and since your net gain is over $250,000, you will be taxed on the remaining $100,000 you gained from selling your home, but not the first $250,000. If you do not meet all of those qualifications, you do not have to worry about the tax.

The rationale behind this is that for Medicare taxes, there is no cap on the wage amount from which the tax is taken, meaning that everyone has Medicare taxes taken out. However, without this tax, people whose incomes come mostly from passive sources, like investments, and not their wages would otherwise not be fairly taxed for Medicare.

CHAPTER 28
INVESTING IN REAL ESTATE WITH LITTLE OR NO MONEY DOWN

Real Estate is a business that brings you cash in very small time possible. People usually withdraw from the idea because of the initial cash investment involved. But if you are really willing to adopt real estate as your professions then there are certainly ways in which you can invest in real estate without money. Especially in economic recession time it is a feasible option to invest in something with no money down. The various ways in which this can be done are as follows:

Seller Financing

Using this method when buying a property you can seek out potential sellers who are willing to finance you. Usually sellers who want to get rid of their property and are in no hurry to get the cash will allow for this for a longer period of time. If you do not have enough cash to invest, then you must look out for such sellers. The repayment term can be as long as 25 years depending on the seller. Longer the repayment for you, it will be more beneficial for you. You will need sharp skills to be able to convince the seller for this kind of financing.

Selling and Buying Simultaneously

This is a very useful method must requires you to be very smart, quick and proficient. It depends on buying the property and then immediately selling it with a little markup. You do not need much investment for this. You can ask the seller for some time to do the complete payment and in the mean time you find a buyer who is ready to take the property with immediate payment. Although there is a little markup through this method, it ensures the continuity of the business.

Getting yourself a Partner

One of the very helpful and long terms investment way is to find a business partner who is also willing to start up with real estate. Make sure that whatever partner you select for yourself has enough money to invest on the real estate business. You can have your friend or relative or anyone as your partner but makes sure whoever you select is trustworthy and reliable. You must make an agreement governing the principles of your partnership and ascertain that both the partners stick to it.

Mortgages

Another way is that you can take over the seller's mortgages payment i.e. assuming the mortgage. This only applies to mortgaged places, if you are buying one. The original lender must give his approval in this regard. Alongside taking the original mortgage you can get a second mortgage from the seller for the rest of the payment. You can offer the seller terms that will sound beneficial to him like high interest and short term payment.

Free Rent

You can offer different benefits to the seller instead of down payment. One of this is to give them a portion of house free of rental costs for some year's time that will equal the down payment.

Although there are various different methods can be used in real investment with little money, everyone is not able to manage it as it requires high degree of hard work, patience and persistence.

CHAPTER 29
A CREATIVE METHOD FOR INVESTING IN REAL ESTATE WITH LITTLE OR NO MONEY DOWN

Real estate is a business that guarantees huge profits in a comparatively lesser period of time but most people shy away from real estate dealings because they think that in order to enter the real estate business they need to invest a lot of money. The notion is true to some extent but if you are creative in your approach you can actually enter the real estate game without having to invest very little or no money of your own.

One of the ways of undertaking a real estate financing activity for the purpose of making money without investing your own money is seller financing.

Seller Financing

Seller financing is a very popular kind of real estate investment. The best thing about seller financing is that it is beneficial, in its own unique way, to both the owner of the property and the buyer of that property. The first question that comes to your mind regarding this phenomenon is: Why will a seller finance the sale of his own house? What's in it for him?

In this mode of property transaction, the seller of the property himself becomes the lender. The terms and conditions of the sale are agreed upon by both the parties. What essentially happens is that the seller agrees to take the payment not in a lump sum. Rather the payment is spread over an agreed period of time. The seller can also charge mark-up.

If you are going for seller financing, make sure that you have checked the repayment schedule and the terms & conditions are acceptable to you. If possible, ask a lawyer friend or acquaintance to review the deal for you. It will be very beneficial

There are various reasons that might make an owner go for seller financing. Some of them are stated below:

Higher price - An owner could opt for seller financing simply for the reason that it fetches him relatively higher price. The buyer, on his part, agrees to pay a higher price because it gets them easier terms and conditions. Another reason is that if in the future, the buyer decides to sell - he can sell the contract and collect cash.

Higher returns - Seller financing enables a buyer to get higher returns on his amount when he decides to sell. The return is spread over along period of time and guarantees continuous cash flow to the owner.

Faster sale - Seller financing enables an owner to sell his property in the shortest possible time because he is not asking cash payment. In fact he is facilitating the deal by offering help to the buyer of the house. Buyers usually go for such sales in which they do not need to stuck-up their cash.

A great option for selling - If a person has a certain property that is proving difficult to sell through conventional ways, he may find this method very alluring. Seller financing allows a seller to get his asking price. Though he is also forced to make some concessions regarding terms and conditions of sale. But there are various buyers who are willing to pay the asking price in return for easier terms and conditions.

With seller financing a buyer can search those sellers who are willing to finance him. Usually these are people who want to get rid of their property but are not in urgent need of cash. They can usually defer the payment over a longer period of time. If you are short of initial cash for investment, you should look out for people who are willing to extend seller financing facility. The longer the period of time, the more feasible it will be for you.

CHAPTER 30
WAYS OF INVESTING IN REAL ESTATE WITH LITTLE OR NO MONEY DOWN

Do you want to invest in the real estate business and the only thing that is stopping you from starting this venture is your inability to generate the necessary amount of cash or financing? There are ways available for investing in real estate with little or no down money. You just need to be a little bit creative in you approach and familiarize yourself with certain methods of investing that are unusual yet effective.

Real estate is one of the most lucrative and profitable business yet most people shy away form it because they think that real estate investment requires a great deal of capital. That initial capital remains tied up in a property until it is sold. The profits come only after the sale is through. A lot of people do not want to part with their money for such a long time. The return is not guaranteed either. You can sell the property after three months and still lose money. Such apprehensions make it impossible for a layman to enter the real estate business.

What if there were ways in which you could invest in real estate with very little of your own money?

Any successful investor will testify to the fact that an investor does not necessarily have to cough up all the cash needed for a transaction. You may not believe it at first. But it is very much possible. There are several ways in which you can invest in real estate with little or no down money. Some of these methods are stated below:

Double Escrow

If you have previously been involved in a real estate deal, you must have been aware of the escrow account. There is such a term as double escrow. The process means buying and selling a certain piece pf property at roughly the same time. In short, you buy a property from someone and request him to delay receipt of payment for a few days. Within that time, you find a buyer for the same property and sell it to him on a different price. The money that you receive from the buyer is used to pay the seller. The difference amount is your profit. If you are going for a double escrow deal, you must make sure that you already have a buyer of the property, before you finalize the deal with the seller.

Owner's Existing Financing

You can use the existing financing of the property seller for your own deal. When a property owner puts up his home for sale, he usually already has a financing. You can convince him that you will assume his mortgage for a certain amount of time - until the house is sold. At that point you can use the money from sale to service the mortgage - the rest of the amount is your profit.

Taking in Partners

The current crisis has hit most of the people. The catch is that it has not hit everyone. There are still people who have lots of cash. Since the prices of real estate have fallen dramatically, it is the best time for them to buy properties. These properties can be sold later at exponential prices. You can find such persons who are loaded with cash and make them business partners - of course you can offer a percentage of your profit. Since most of the people have little or no experience of the real estate business, they will be more the willing to be your partners.

Apart from the above mentioned methods, there are more options available for a willing individual to make lots of money in the real estate market with little or no down money. You just need to be an effective negotiator and a hardworking individual with a creative approach towards money making.

Buying Mortgages

Buying mortgaged properties is also one of the most feasible options for investing in real estate with no money down. There are many people nowadays who are willing to shed off their mortgaged properties. There is just one technicality involved in his process. You need approval of the original lender whether he has no objection to your taking up the mortgage.

Partnership

Most probably, you are pressed for cash at this moment. But right at thins moment, there are other people who are loaded with it. These people have lots of money but they have no business acumen so their money lies in their banks earning them minimum profit. You find and make such a person your partner. Such a person, who has lots of liquidity available, can help you in more ways that you can imagine. But what's in it for him? He can make good use of his money and get better returns. You can also offer him a share of your profits.

Before you take in a partner, make sure that he is an honest person. He should, preferably, be a person who has previously worked with you in one or the other capacity. Such a person will be suitable to get along with and you will be very unlikely to counter any problems later in your relationship.

CHAPTER 31
TIPS TO BUY A HOME WITH LITTLE OR NO MONEY OF YOUR OWN

S uccessful investors understand the importance of the availability of capital to pursue the beneficial real estate investments and grow their business. This capital need not come from their savings. No investor puts their hard earned money to new big deals requiring big investments. An experienced investor will try every possible method to get the required amount financed on the most favorable terms. These methods are possible not only for the big investors but also for the small home buyers. You too could act like an experienced investor and purchase your dream home without any down payment or paying very little. You should follow some tips to purchase a home without paying anything.

Hire an attorney before signing the agreement

Do not rub your head in understanding the meaning of the terms of the bank or financial institution but it is advisable to hire an attorney and let him review your agreement or contract. The review of the agreement or contract is necessary and should be done before you put sign on the important papers. The review by the attorney would protect your interests in the deal.

Pay cash advance

Cash is king in the real estate contract and so if you can immediately pay cash to the sellers then they will prefer to deal with you. Cash payment can win you the race with many other investors who are running to reach the same target. Tell your sellers that you want to pay cash and they will forget the other competitive offers. By paying cash, you can ask for the relaxation and the relaxation offered to you will be your profit. You can pay cash to secure your dream home but consult with your attorney and include the details in the agreement also.

Manage sources for the investment

To pay cash, you need regular source of investment and to get the required investment you should try those sources where you will have to pay the least interest. For example, if you take money from your friends or family members then they may not charge you any interest or very less interest but if you cannot manage funds from your family members and friends then go to professionals. Ask those banks or financial institutions for the investment that are reputed and offering the required amount at the least interest rates.

Partner with the sellers

If you meet any seller who need money but also want to retain his ownership then you can partner with such a homeowner and in return you will get percentage of ownership. In future if the market share of your property rises then you can either purchase it fully or sell your partnership either to the seller or someone else to make profit on your investment.

CHAPTER 32
REAL ESTATE INVESTING - MAKE MONEY IN REAL ESTATE WITH LITTLE OR NO MONEY

It's a contemporary notion that in order to succeed in the real estate business, you must have a lot of money. The concept is only partially true. Money can be made in the real estate market with having to invest lots of it. You might conclude that if money is not that essential, maybe you need to have a handsome financing facility or suitable asset to use as collateral. Again, I will tell you that even those are not necessary for starting your real estate business. What I am about to tell you is not a short cut to riches. Infact, you can make a career out of it. The concept that I am talking about is called wholesaling. In order to become a wholesaler you do not need to have lots of cash. Infact, you don't need to have a good credit rating either.

What is wholesaling?

Wholesaling means finding a seller who is willing to sell his property for a slightly lesser amount than its current market value. The next part is to find buyers for the same property and sell it at a good price. The key to success in this field is the wholesaler's communication skills and his ability to market his property aggressively.

If you have the necessary skills, you can become a successful wholesaler and make a few grand on every sale with no down money of your own.. Wholesaling needs a few skills. Some of them are listed below.

Finding and locating good property

The most effective way of finding a good property is to drive around the neighborhood and keep your eyes open. You can also scan internet listing sites or the classified sections but the actual survey of a location and on-the-ground inspection of proposed sites is way better than browsing locations on the net.

Ever heard the saying: birds of a feather fly together? In order to get into the real estate game you should surround yourself with people who are already into this business. If you are moving in a circle of real estate investors and agents there is a strong possibility that you will get to know about possible investment venues is by the word of mouth.

118

Tune up your interpersonal skills

What a wholesaler actually does it to persuade a seller to sell his property to him. This needs cutting edge inter-personal skills since it takes a lot of convincing to make someone sell his property to you at a discount. Actually this is the real job of the wholesaler.

The genius to sell

You can buy all the properties at your desired price but if you don't have buyers for those properties the sum total of all your efforts will be zero. In order to get potential buyers to contact you, get your property advertised in the classified ads. Also spread the message around within your circle that you have great properties for sale. You are sure to get calls from potential buyers. Keep record of all such buyers since you will need them for your next assignment. It is better to establish working relationship with these customers so that whenever you come across a great property you have a ready -made pool of buyers to choose from. It is essential that every one in your circle knows that you are in the real estate business.

When will you start making money?

I wrote earlier in this book that this is not a quick-rich short-cut. The process will take time and patience. In the initial stages you may encounter some difficulties but with consistence and perseverance, you will acquire the essential skills for this business.

CHAPTER 33
NO MONEY DOWN - HOW TO BUY PROPERTY WITH NOTHING DOWN

One thing I must mention first, however, is that ANY information, combined with NO action, produces NO result. If I came over to your house and showed you everything in person and answered all of your questions, and then you did NOTHING.....it was a waste of time. Yours and mine!! On the other hand, if you combine information with hard work, persistence and, most of all, GUTS, you will be successful, whether you buy the courses, read the books for free at the library, or get the information from me, right here!

I mentioned GUTS because there's a price to be paid for everything. If you had a million dollars, you could buy an apartment building without hardly any difficulty. Just pick out one that you liked, had a good return, and passed a building inspection.

If you DON'T have a million dollars, what are you to do? Well get ready for some hard work, searching for the right deal. Get ready to have a whole slew of offers rejected, and maybe even laughed at. Get ready to hear some pompous real estate agent tell you (as one told me) "Son, I've been in the real estate business for thirty years now, and let me tell you, there's no such thing as a no money down deal." Get ready to work on a deal and spend time on it only to have it collapse.

You're going to put in your down payment in the form of "brain sweat equity". You're going to pay by acquiring more knowledge than others in the area of creative real estate, and by searching long and hard to find MOTIVATED sellers, ones who want to get rid of their properties desperately and therefore are willing to help you out. Most of all, you're going to pay by enduring the inevitable "start-up glitches" that ANY business or enterprise has. If it was easy to do, then everybody would be doing it, and there would be no properties left! It is this difficulty that makes it EASY, once you know what you are doing!!

OK, so here we go, but first you need to know ONE thing: IN REAL ESTATE EVERYTHING IS NEGOTIABLE!! Let me say that again, because it is the linchpin of the way creative real estate works--in real estate EVERYTHING is negotiable!

What does that mean? Are there any boundaries? NO!!

Can you get someone to carry an agreement for sale for 25 years with little or no money down and no credit check? YES!! Are there ten ads in the paper offering just such an agreement, or one? Probably none! What does that mean? EVERYTHING is negotiable! If you find a motivated seller, one who is paying every month to own that property, one who doesn't have the skills to fix it up, one who moved out of town, or the country, then he MIGHT go for it! Notice that I did not say WILL go for it, but MIGHT!

Think of yourself when you had a car that you wanted to get rid of, because it was a piece of junk. If someone approached you and asked "how much?", you'd say "$1000, firm". But you knew deep inside that you just wanted to get rid of the headache!! And if you ever had to wait for a month or two with no one buying your car, suddenly you were not quite so firm on the price! And if the alternator had to be replaced before the car could run, pretty soon you just wanted it OUT of your hands!! NOW, you're ready to accept monthly payments, maybe hold something as security, etc. You just want it GONE!

It is the same with real estate properties! They go from being our pride and joy to an albatross around our necks--then we're ready to do WHATEVER it takes to get rid of it!

These people aren't going to jump up and down and say "I'm willing to take a no money down deal for my property"! They are going to be depressed, just like the fellow with a clunker in his back yard, sitting there for months. They are going to need some convincing, but if you find the "DON'T WANTER", the most difficult part is done! Then you make offers, look closely at each property to see if you can make a go of it (that's a whole other report!) if you can get the property--sometimes you don't want it either! Then it is just a matter of making offers, either in person, or through a realtor, until you find someone who is

ready to deal. The first time is the hardest, because no matter how many times I tell you (or the TV guys) that it CAN be done, you are going to think "not for me, not here in _____, not any more, not with my areas laws and zoning regulations, not with my personality, not with my brains, etc."

Don't you believe it! Look at all the people in the TV commercials-all types and shapes-they have ONE thing in common--they went out and DID IT!

ALL IT TAKES IS GUTS AND PERSEVERANCE!!

Here's the "stream of consciousness" of ideas on how to buy with $000.00 down, but keep in mind the whole time that IN REAL ESTATE EVERYTHING IS

NEGOTIABLE!

1) The simplest way to buy with no money down is to get the seller to carry an agreement for sale. Monthly payments for 25 years are possible if the seller has no need for the money, and can be convinced to get his 6,7,8% return secured by his house instead of buying a 4% bond.

2) If you have good credit and want to put no money into a property, try a first mortgage, Vendor carries a big second for remainder. Seller gets , say 75%, and carries 25%.

3) Again with good credit, try first, smaller 2nd, and a Personal Line of Credit for remainder--especially if the gap is only $10-15,000. This can even work for low priced properties where the first mortgage is combined with a PLC for the remainder--be smart enough to go to another bank for PLC and tell them that you're going to make an invstment with money--and don't tell ANY bank that you're doing a no money down deal!

4) Payment over time-seller wants $5,000 down, for example. How about $400 per month for a year? You're still paying it, but over time-maybe the property will generate enough extra money to pay this!

5) Back taxes-I've done deals where I've taken over back taxes due--you can pay them off at your own speed,

within reason!

6) Free rent-I've done deals where the seller had office space in the building and took 2 years free rent as down payment! Can also work for multi family.

7) Upon closing there are adjustments for that months rent--close on the 2nd or 3rd to maximize this-and for damage deposits, taxes to be paid for the period owned by seller, utility bills to be paid, etc. These can add up to a large amount!

8) Since the bank starts mortgage payments one month from closing, simply by paying an interest adjustment of 2 weeks allows you to use the first months rent and apply the second months rent to the mortgage payment.

9) Borrow on insurance policy, stocks, bonds, mutual funds, etc. If you allow the bank to secure the collateral they will be very accommodating.

10) Rack up your Visa, Mastercard and American Expres cards. A bit crazy, but I assume its a great investment!

11) Borrow from friends, relatives, boss (holiday pay?) Maybe even cut them in as partners!

12) Partners are a surefire way to get accepted for big bank loans, create enough down payments, etc. Always look for people who are interested in this area, and ask

them what prevents them from buying investment properties. If its time, expertise, etc--then you have a fit! All that's preventing you is money--and you have found this great property haven't you?

13) Syndicate a group of people--say 9 investors and you get the last tenth for putting together the project--they will provide the financial strength for the loan, and maybe even the down payments! Anything is possible, remember? This is a lot of work to find these people, but VERY lucrative! Start with dentists and doctors, lawyers, everyone that you deal with!

14) Rent to buy--maybe you make payments for 3 years and then have built up the downpayment-- meanwhile the property can go up in value, rents rise, and so on.

15) Option to buy--Seller keeps title and gets all revenue. You simply pay a sum for the right (make it REALLY legal!) to purchase the property at a certain sum in X years. There could be a trade for this option, example trade an item or service for the option.

16) Lets make trading an item or service for down payment its own idea!

17) Foreclosure property--maybe just before it goes into foreclosure you offer to keep up the payments and give seller SOMETHING, SOMETIME for his equity.

(In a short while he's not getting anything!) Lots of work, lots of books and announcement services available.

18) Fix up damaged property--work deal with bank-- example: as is it's worth $75,000, with clean up and fix up its worth 100,000--bank offers 75,000 mortgage based on future value--you have to do fix up--similar to sweat equity.

19) Lease property (ie an office building) from owner and sub lease it to tennants--must be very legal and usually needs strong rent up effort!

20) Pay someone to cosign for a loan

21) Get realtor to carry his commission as a note--they HATE this, but if its needed..

22) Balloon payment--nothing down, balance due in three years

23)Private money from mortgage brokers--ask them about it! High rate of interest, but..

24) Refinance property either before you assume it, or after

25) Find a partner where he takes writeoff for negative cash flow and you manage property--this can even work with buying your personal residence--investor is happy with $200 per month negative cash flow in return for your taking care of property, always a tennant (you) and

investor splits profit when selling.

That's going to be enough to start some gears running in your head. The most important part is to keep trying, and to be creative. Combining parts of one idea and another, and always probing for what the seller wants will lead you to solutions. Always probe for ways to make both of you happy. Everyone wants all cash, right now-- not everyone gets it! Think of the junker car in the back yard and look for ways to HELP the other person--they want to sell!

Most of all, keep looking! It is not a failure on your part if someone is clinging to the hope that they'll get a certain price, or certain terms. If they can-great!! If not, check back in a few months. Many properties are still sitting there and with a MUCH more receptive seller after they have the property "sitting in their backyard, rusting" (or racking up negative cash flow and maintenance and property management headaches). Try and try again!

CHAPTER 34
STRATEGY BY THE NUMBERS

The following is a simple step-by-step process for creating a strategic plan by the numbers. This is a ten step process that can be used by a group, an organization, or an individual.

1) Twenty-one questions

Brainstorm to make a list of the first twenty-one challenges that come to mind. This can be done as a group, or as an individual. Ideas should be based primarily on identified opportunities to improve, real current challenges, or competitive necessities. Brainstorming means a free flow of ideas, so do not discourage or debate the merit of any individual ideas until twenty-one items have been identified.

If you are experiencing difficulty in identifying a list of twenty-one issues or ideas for improvements, then try using a SWOT Analysis. The SWOT Analysis is a list of your strengths, weaknesses, opportunities, and threats. This can help to give perspective and spark some ideas, but may not be necessary to identify a quick list of twenty-one issues, obstacles, problems, and opportunities.

Once you have created a list of twenty-one suggestions, stop. The list is complete. The first twenty-one ideas that come to mind are the most important opportunities and the most relevant issues. Anything beyond the top twenty-one ideas is getting too detailed in the issues, and can wait for the next strategic planning session.

2) Assign a point value to your twenty-one ideas

Review your list of twenty-one potential issues and opportunities, and assign points based on the following criteria.

Assign one point to each idea that is important. Important means long term and lasting benefit that truly impacts or changes the business. Be honest about your assessment.

Assign one point to each idea that is urgent. Urgent means that the idea or improvement needs to be implemented immediately, because waiting would have catastrophic consequences.

Assign up to three points based on your determination of the benefit. Benefit can be measured as financial benefit, or customer satisfaction benefit, or some other metric of benefit. Whatever methodology is used to determine benefit, this same measurement must be applied to all twenty-one ideas. For example, if you choose to use financial impact as the measurement for benefit, then all twenty-one items should be measured by financial impact. Do not mix and match, as with measuring some items by financial benefit, and measuring others by customer satisfaction impact. The metric should be the same for all ideas. The value of three applies to significant realistic benefit. The value of two applies to significant benefit, but not really sure if it can be achieved. The value of one applies if the benefit can probably be achieved, but may not be significant. If the benefit is not significant, and not likely to be achieved, then it is reasonable not to award any points for the idea, and move on to the next idea on the list.

Assign up to three points based on your ability to affect change, implement the idea, or address the issue. If you are absolutely certain that this is within your control to do, then assign a value of three. If you feel that it can be done with some concentrated effort, then assign a value of two, If it can be done, but requires resources, investment, budget, or other assistance to get the job done, then assign a value of one.

Add up the points assigned to each idea. Now you have a score for each suggestion,

3) Pick the Lucky Seven

Sort and prioritize the ideas based on the total score for

each suggestion, from high score to low score.

The seven ideas with the highest points are the lucky seven that will get your attention. In the event of a tie score, agree on the final seven. Review the final list one more time and confirm your top seven priorities. The other fourteen ideas are really good suggestions, and may be the starting point for your next strategic planning session. For now, we will only focus on the top seven.

4) Ask the Five "Why's"

One by one, for each of the lucky seven selected ideas, ask the question "Why" five times. First, ask, "Why?" When you have the answer to that question, ask the same question about your answer. For example, "This idea will help me improve customer satisfaction." "Why?" "Because this is something that customers are always asking for." "Why?" "They are frustrated by not knowing what to expect." "Why?" "They have no visibility to our schedule, status, or progress." "Why?" "Our ETA is not always the same. We cannot communicate an expected completion date, and there is no method to give them updates." "Why?" "Creating a way to give updates would have some development cost, and it would take time to design the customer interface."

Some individuals may become frustrated asking "Why" five times. The reason that it can be frustrating is that the answer may appear to be abundantly clear as common sense. Even though the answer may appear obvious, it is still beneficial to ask the question, and dig a little deeper into relevance and root cause. In the example above, it is not enough to know that the idea will improve customer satisfaction, but by asking the question "why" five times, it created some additional clarity with regards to the real customer value and the real underlying obstacles. Practice asking the question "why" five times, even if you need to slightly adjust the question or the answer to give yourself an opportunity to dig a little deeper into each idea.

When you have completed asking the question "why" five times for each question, it is time to asses your lucky seven ideas. After this further review and assessment, you can decide if you want to work on all lucky seven opportunities and issues, of if you want to work on just a few of them. The magic number that you choose is based on what you feel that you can handle, based on your assessment of each opportunity.

5) Assign your METRICS

Measure Everything That Results In Customer Satisfaction. Identify two primary metrics for each of the ideas that you have selected to pursue. These two primary metrics will be the method to compare past history, and future success. Things that get measured get done.

The first metric is based on the goal that you wish to impact or achieve. Metrics must be tangible items that can be measured with a numerical, financial, or date assignment. For example, a reasonable metric is to reduce cost, increase revenue, increase profit, decrease hours or time to complete a task, decrease time to obtain a response, increase production by a predetermined percentage, etc. If it is a good idea, then find a way to measure progress and assign a goal.

The second metric is based on a measurement that could potentially be adversely affected by the attainment of the goal for the primary metric. For example, if the primary metric is to reduce time, a secondary metric may be to measure the associated cost to achieve the goal. If a primary metric is to reduce price, a secondary metric may be to measure the impact to quality as determined by number of defects. Consider the potential undesired consequences of achieving your primary metric, and assign a secondary metric as your control. The combination on these two metrics will greatly enhance your success.

6) Create your schedule

Identify key tasks and milestones associated with your ideas and implementing improvements. Perhaps you have commitments for dates, or a fiscal period that must be accommodated. Perhaps you are in a competitive race for the solution. Perhaps you have an idea of the project plan and key milestones for implementation. Use your judgment to assign a tentative schedule for achieving your metrics. The schedule may be subject to change upon further review, but it is important to recognize important commitments and establish expectations.

7) Do it

Create a plan for each objective and implement it. The process for creating an implementation plan for each idea is distinctly different from the strategic planning process.

8) Measure it

Measure your results, both the primary metric and the control metric. How did you do compared to your goal?

9) Learn from the experience and make adjustments

Use the knowledge that you have gained from the experience as a review before beginning the next strategic planning session. It may create new opportunities, and it may help to refine your perspective for other ideas.

10) Go back to the first step It is time to start planning again

Wash, rinse, and repeat.

Words of Wisdom

"There is a theory which states that if ever anybody discovers exactly what the Universe is for and why it is here, it will instantly disappear and be replaced by something even more bizarre and inexplicable. There is another theory which states that this has already happened."

- Douglas Adams

"Why be a man when you can be a success?"

- Bertolt Brecht

"An economist is an expert who will know tomorrow why the things he predicted yesterday didn't happen today."

- Lawrence J. Peter

CHAPTER 35
MAKE SURE YOU'RE USING 2 OR 3 EXIT STRATEGIES

Real estate investors who jump in with both feet and buy a home inexpensively might think they've got a great deal. But they don't. Technically, they don't have a great deal until they can turn around and make money on that property. Making money on owned property is called "exiting" and there are numerous ways you can do it. Before you buy a property you should make sure that you have 2 or 3 different exit strategies in place for various circumstances. Here are a few options to consider:

Exit strategy #1 - Buy and hold: When you buy a property and hold it, you are waiting for it to appreciate. This was a strategy when house prices were climbing, although many investors don't feel like this is going to happen any time soon. However, buying low right now might be the best choice if you feel that house prices will climb again in the future!

Exit strategy #2 - Landlording: Although you're not technically exiting from the purchase of the property, you are still benefiting from ongoing rental revenue so it is included in an exit strategy.

Exit strategy #3 - Flip: If you want to earn fast cash, flip the house to another investor or to a landlord. When you do this, you probably won't charge full market value for the home but instead offer it at a discount so that someone else can buy the house and do something with it while you walk away with a small profit.

Exit strategy #4 - Sell: Even though the market is in rough shape, people are still buying houses. You can buy your home at an inexpensive price and resell it for full market value to consumers.

Don't go into your real estate investing without thinking of at least 2 exit strategies for every home. By considering more than one, you'll be able to be flexible should you find that the market shifts unexpectedly. Mix and match the exit strategies - for example, buy the home, landlord it for a while, then flip it over to a landlord who might appreciate getting a home with tenants.

Having exit strategies will help you feel more confident during your investing and will ensure that you are more likely to earn an income from your effort.

CHAPTER 36
THE NEW ECONOMY REAL ESTATE MODEL - A SOFT SELL CONCEPT

As far back as the 1970's Sears envisioned a kiosk in their stores where a customer could buy stock and even real estate. It was a bold look at the future from one of the world's largest retailers. All they had to do was to get the consumer to come to their stores to do business. This was quite a challenge thrown down to both Wall Street and Main Street USA. Most of us probably never heard or remember this strategy, and it never got off the ground. People just did not equate Sears with stock or real estate; they were a department store.

In fairness to Sears, the technologies and conveniences did not exist to enable the plan. Sears may have also thought themselves too big to fail. That theme does seem to be a constant.

Hmm, it appears that history does indeed repeat itself, and perhaps at shorter and shorter intervals. It may be ironic that by speeding up processes and the rate at which things can change, the lessons of history are lost at a quicker rate. Did that make sense? If it did, you may be thinking a bit like me - you've been cautioned.

In the 1980's the successful real estate agent became more independent and needed fewer and fewer services from the brokerage firm. As they claimed a higher and higher portion of the brokerage fee, margins for the real estate brokerage began to shrink. Some phenomenally high interest rates had a similar impact on the mortgage banking industry. Unless buyers had no choice, they did not take on these inflated mortgages. The mortgage industry literally shrunk along with their profit margins. We all know that real estate cycles; it goes up and it goes down. The curve is rarely smooth, and is punctuated by sharp turns in one direction or another. Most features of the real estate industry react quickly to the conditions in the market that affect it. Now we have the background for the next attempt to create a commodities market from the real estate process.

In 1974, the Real Estate Settlement and Procedures Act (RESPA), as amended, was passed. It opened the door for consolidations within the industry. To foster competition, companies were regulated to prevent abuses in the industry and to keep prices to the consumer lower. It was almost ironic that the very act that was passed to prevent abuses, in a way opened the door. I don't know that it has empirically been demonstrated that RESPA actually lowered costs or prevented abuses. With HUD as a watchdog, there was little real enforcement, and although fines were levied, industry practices ultimately were left to the states to manage. It took decades to sort it out, and Wall Street only a few months to make it yesterday's issue.

The point for mentioning RESPA was that it allowed what was called "controlled business entities," a term later changed to "affiliated business entities." The home builder and the real estate brokerage could now have a captive mortgage and title business. The theory was that this would somehow create efficiencies and economies lowering the cost and improve service to the consumer. It didn't. With all of this vertical integration, each one of the independently managed businesses was caught in the same financial wringer.

What was not taken into consideration was the pro-cyclical nature of the model. When one business was down so were the others. The upside was champagne and roses, but the downside left little room for beer and carnations. There were other oversights as well. Not understanding the risk models for businesses outside of their core competencies was seldom given the focus it deserved. Few also embraced managing the business with the same zeal they had for their core model.

142

The result was that many of these affiliated arrangements have failed, and the industry model for how transactions are managed remains much the same as it has since the post WWII era. Certainly technology has improved systems, but not nearly to the extent that it could. The competitive natures of the individual sectors of the real estate business keep the technologies proprietary and therefore parochial. A 21st Century model for the industry will come from somewhere outside of the core real estate industry. Next came a far a more organized and systematic attempt to create a commodity market in the real estate arena.

The boldest strategy to commoditize the residential real estate market came from a company called National Realty Trust (NRT). NRT has gone through a number of name changes. In the mid to late 1990s NRT was known as Cendant (CD). The CEO of Cendant, Henry Silverman was a Wall Street visionary who understood commodities. He was big in the rental car business (Avis) and in hospitality with a string of motel franchises. Mr. Silverman viewed the real estate as a commodity that could be franchised and methodically went about acquiring national real estate marks such as Coldwell Banker (Residential), Century 21, ERA and Sotheby's. Subsequently they also acquired established regional real estate companies. They were and remain the largest single group of real estate companies in the industry.

Cendant experienced an accounting scandal in the last decade and lost its impetus. It never quite recovered from the scandal, and the company divided its assets into four groups. The real estate companies were sold to the Apollo Management Group. Apollo has been beset by the soft real estate market and a suit filed by Carl Icahn over a debt exchange plan. With the continuing financial and legal problems, they stumble along with business as usual. They are not in a position to lead the real estate industry into the 21st Century. This strategy involved getting in upstream in the transaction by "owning" the gatekeeper function. It required enormous amounts of capital, and technology was evolving to provide a far more efficient less capital intensive platform to emerge. The Internet makes anyone with the vision and the concept to be a potential player.

CHAPTER 37
SOME CONSIDERATIONS ON THE FOR SALE BY OWNER REAL ESTATE SALES CHANNEL

F or Sale By Owner is a sales channel whereby the property owner, himself, is selling his own property-for-sale. The most common practice in real estate selling is that a property owner courses his for-sale-property to an accredited agent or broker. The broker will be fully responsible for the marketing, closing of sale, sales legal documentation and even after sales care, in trade of a commission percentage.

Hence, sales in this channel, frees the property owner from all the hassles and nitty-gritty details of the entire sales transactions. However, a number of property owners still opt to do the selling themselves for various reasons; it might be due to some financial considerations, personal inhibitions or any other reasons of personal logic. Such sales channel of personal selling of one's property is duly acceptable but entails some downside considerations:

Limited Marketing Network

Selling a real estate property entails an effective marketing strategy and networking to acquire the best deal possible. Personal selling of one's property, undoubtedly, is more arduous than when it is channelled through an authorized real estate professional broker. For one, personal selling has a limited network of prospective buyers; whereas, professional real estate brokers have their own marketing networks which can directly provide them a string of prospective buyers.

Sales and Documentation Procedure Expertise

With the exception that the property owner is a real estate professional, it is much to one's advantage to course through the selling of his property to a licensed real estate broker. A simple property owner without any real estate trading negotiation background or expertise would literally be groping in the entire sales and sales legal documentation procedures. Closing the sale for a property is just the tip of the entire sales process.

After the deal has been sealed and closed, comes the detailed sales documentation which practically involves the submission of a long list of valid documentary requirements to be submitted to respective housing agencies and other government legal offices to fully consummate the sale. This process is too tedious for somebody who is not familiar with the real estate sector. If the property owner/seller himself is not well-versed with these procedure, then lies the danger of being entangled with the complexities of legal proceedings and thus extending the entire sales negotiation to a longer time.

Emotional investment interference

Emotional investment interferes with the sales negotiations. Real estate properties are personal investments. Often, property owners are very much attached with their owned-property; especially if it was acquired from hard-earned money and even blood money, for some. This often deters the immediate selling of the property to an interested buyer whose characteristics are not within the ideals of the property owner/personal seller. Whereas, a real estate agent or broker would not be as sensitive to these considerations when selling a property because what matters most is that the property will be disposed at the right price.

The bottomline of any property-for-sale is the disposal of such property at the best package price, in whatever sales channel available. However, the decision of what sales channel to avail is still under the sole discretion of the disposing owner. Whether its For Sale By Owner or For Sale by Agent, the important thing is that at the end of the day, the property will be marked SOLD!

CHAPTER 38
TOP 7 MISTAKES ROOKIE
REAL ESTATE AGENTS MAKE

Every time I talk to someone about my business and career, it always comes up that "they've thought about getting into real estate" or know someone who has. With so many people thinking about getting into real estate, and getting into real estate - why aren't there more successful Realtors in the world? Well, there's only so much business to go around, so there can only be so many Real Estate Agents in the world. I feel, however, that the inherent nature of the business, and how different it is from traditional careers, makes it difficult for the average person to successfully make the transition into the Real Estate Business. As a Broker, I see many new agents make their way into my office - for an interview, and sometimes to begin their careers. New Real Estate Agents bring a lot of great qualities to the table - lots of energy and ambition - but they also make a lot of common mistakes. Here are the 7 top mistakes rookie Real Estate Agents Make.

1) No Business Plan or Business Strategy

So many new agents put all their emphasis on which

Real Estate Brokerage they will join when their shiny new license comes in the mail. Why? Because most new Real Estate Agents have never been in business for themselves - they've only worked as employees. They, mistakenly, believe that getting into the Real Estate business is "getting a new job." What they're missing is that they're about to go into business for themselves. If you've ever opened the doors to ANY business, you know that one of the key ingredients is your business plan. Your business plan helps you define where you're going, how you're getting there, and what it's going to take for you to make your real estate business a success. Here are the essentials of any good business plan:

A) Goals - What do you want? Make them clear, concise, measurable, and achievable.

B) Services You Provide - you don't want to be the "jack of all trades & master of none" - choose residential or commercial, buyers/sellers/renters, and what area(s) you want to specialize in. New residential real estate agents tend to have the most success with buyers/renters and then move on to listing homes after they've completed a few transactions.

C) Market - who are you marketing yourself to?

D) Budget - consider yourself "new real estate agent, inc." and write down EVERY expense that you have -

gas, groceries, cell phone, etc... Then write down the new expenses you're taking on - board dues, increased gas, increased cell usage, marketing (very important), etc...

E) Funding - how are you going to pay for your budget w/ no income for the first (at least) 60 days? With the goals you've set for yourself, when will you break even?

F) Marketing Plan - how are you going to get the word out about your services? The MOST effective way to market yourself is to your own sphere of influence (people you know). Make sure you do so effectively and systematically.

2) Not Using the Best Possible Closing Team

They say the greatest businesspeople surround themselves with people that are smarter than themselves. It takes a pretty big team to close a transaction - Buyer's Agent, Listing Agent, Lender, Insurance Agent, Title Officer, Inspector, Appraiser, and sometimes more! As a Real Estate Agent, you are in the position to refer your client to whoever you choose, and you should make sure that anyone you refer in will be an asset to the transaction, not someone who will bring you more headache. And the closing team you refer in, or "put your name to," are there to make you shine! When they perform well, you get to take part of the credit because you referred them into the transaction.

The deadliest duo out there is the New Real Estate Agent & New Mortgage Broker. They get together and decide that, through their combined marketing efforts, they can take over the world! They're both focusing on the right part of their business - marketing - but they're doing each other no favors by choosing to give each other business. If you refer in a bad insurance agent, it might cause a minor hiccup in the transaction - you make a simple phone call and a new agent can bind the property in less than an hour. However, because it typically takes at least two weeks to close a loan, if you use an inexperienced lender, the result can be disastrous! You may find yourself in a position of "begging for a contract extension," or worse, being denied a contract extension.

A good closing team will typically know more than their role in the transaction. Due to this, you can turn to them with questions, and they will step in (quietly) when they see a potential mistake - because they want to help you, and in return receive more of your business. Using good, experienced players for your closing team will help you infinitely in conducting business worthy of MORE business...and best of all, it's free!

3) Not Arming Themselves with the Necessary Tools

Getting started as a Real Estate Agent is expensive. In Texas, the license alone is an investment that will cost between $700 and $900 (not taking into account the amount of time you'll invest.) However, you'll run into even more expenses when you go to arm yourself with the necessary tools of the trade. And don't fool yourself - they are necessary - because your competitors are definitely using every tool to help THEM.

A) MLS Access is probably the most expensive necessity you're going to run into. Joining your local (and state & national, by default) Board of Realtors will allow you to pay for MLS access, and in Austin, Texas, will run around $1000. However, don't skimp in this area. Getting MLS access is one of the most important things you can do. It's what differentiates us from your average salesman - we don't sell homes, we present any of the homes that we have available. With MLS Access, you will have 99% of the homes for sale in your area available to present to your clients.

B) Mobile Phone w/ a Beefy Plan - These days, everyone has a cell phone. But not everyone has a plan that will facilitate the level of use that Real Estate Agents need. Plan on getting at least 2000 minutes per month. You want, and need, to be available to your clients 24/7 - not just nights and weekends.

C) Computer (Preferably a Laptop) - There's no way around it, you have to have a computer & be savvy enough to use email. You would be wise to invest in some business management software, as well. If you'd like to save some money (and who wouldn't) then you can get the client & email management software Thunderbird from http://www.mozilla.com and you can get a free office suite from http://www.openoffice.org The only downside to these programs is that they do not sync with your PDA or Smart Phone. A Laptop is a BIG plus because you'll be able to work from home or on the go. New Real Estate Agents are often surprised by just how much time they spend AWAY from the office, and a laptop helps you stay on top of your work while on the go.

D) Real Estate Friendly Car - You don't have to have a Lexus, but your Miata won't do the trick. Make sure that you have a 4 door car or SUV that is comfortable and presentable. Keep it clean, and for God's sake, don't smoke in it! You're going to spend a LOT of time in your car, and put a lot of miles on it, so if it's fuel efficient, it's a BIG plus. If you're driving a sporty convertible, or still have your KILLER Jeep from college, it's time to trade it in.

4) Lack of Proper Funding

If you've taken the time to create your business plan, than you should definitely have your budget, but I can't stress enough the importance of having and following your budget. However, the budget alone doesn't address the important aspect of funding. 90% of all small businesses fail due to lack of funding. Typically, new agents will want to have 3 months of reserves in savings before taking the leap into full time agency. However, money in the bank isn't the only way to answer the question of funding. Maybe your partner can support you for a certain period of time. You can keep a part-time job that won't interfere with your business as a Real Estate Agent. Many successful waiters make the transition to successful real estate agents with no money in the bank. When you start your new business, don't expect to earn any income for, at the least, 60 days.

5) Refusing to Spend Money on Marketing

Most new Real Estate Agents don't realize that the hardest part of the business is finding the business. Furthermore, they've just shelled out around $2000 for their license and board dues, so the LAST thing they want to do is to spend more money! Again, the problem lies in the lack of understanding that you've just jumped into the Real Estate Business, you haven't taken a new job. And any good businessperson will tell you that how much business you GET is directly correlative to how much you SPEND on marketing. If you choose the right brokerage, then you will get some good inbound leads. However, don't neglect a good, personal marketing campaign from the beginning to get your own name out as the Real Estate Agent to go to.

6) Not Focusing Their Marketing Efforts in the Most Effective Areas

One reason why many new Real Estate Agents who do begin spending money on personal marketing stop is because they spend it in the wrong place. The easiest place, and where conventional Real Estate tells you to spend your money, is in conventional print marketing - the newspaper, real estate magazines, etc... This is the most visible place to see real estate advertising, it's where large offices spend a good part of their money, and so many new agents mistakenly spend their money here. This becomes very frustrating to new agents because of its low return. Large brokerages can afford to spend their money here because they're filling two needs - they're marketing their own properties for sale while creating new buyer traffic for their buyer's agents. New Real Estate Agents should look to their own sphere of influence and referral marketing to see the most effective return on their investment. An agent can spend as little as $100/month marketing to their family, friends, and colleagues and see an incredible return. There are many great referral systems around that all focus on the same premise - that if you consistently market yourself to your

156

sphere of influence as the Real Estate Agent to go to - then you will get more business. The key is to pick a system and to follow that system. You will see results.

7) Choosing the Wrong Brokerage for the Wrong Reasons

New Real Estate Agents choose their new broker for a variety of reasons - they have a good reputation, they offer the most competitive split, the office is close to their house, etc... While these alone aren't bad reasons to choose a broker, they aren't going to do a lot to help you in your success. The #1 reason to choose a broker, and the question to ask is, "What do you offer your new agents." If the answer is, "The most competitive split in town" you should definitely keep looking. Remember, 100% of $0 is still $0. If you're leaning towards the largest broker in town, who has a great reputation, remember this: You're starting a BUSINESS not a JOB. While it might be fantastic to brag to your friends about landing a job at a prestigious company, it's no accomplishment to hang your license on the same wall in the same office as other successful agents.

Your #1 concern when interviewing new Brokers is what they offer you as a new agent. Do they have incoming leads? What does their training program consist of? What's their retention level? What's their average sales price? Do they encourage their agents to promote themselves? A Broker's purpose is to help new agents start successful careers and to help established Agents progress their careers to the next level. As a new agent, concern yourself less with commission split or agency name and more with specific programs and agency standards.

A new career in Real Estate is very exciting. Starting a Real Estate business provides the new Agent with opportunities for limitless potential and freedom. New Agents have a notoriously high failure rate, however, so a new Real Estate career can also be a very scary prospect.

CHAPTER 39
SHOULD YOU LEASE OR BUY YOUR COMMERCIAL REAL ESTATE?

First let's consider the purchase of real estate.

In buying a commercial building you are acquiring an asset that adds substance to the balance sheet. It builds equity over time as the mortgage gets paid off and as the value of the real estate goes up. It is an asset than can be borrowed against in the future or rented for income.

It gives the company a tangible asset which often times ends up being one of the company's largest assets. It can become a large part of a business owner's wealth building and/or retirement strategies.

A nice building can provide the owners of a company with other intangible benefits such as a feeling of stability, control and pride of ownership. A company's building can also be their largest billboard and advertising vehicle. There are no rent increases to be concerned about or any risk of eviction or non-renewal of your lease by the Landlord.

A piece of property strategically acquired can also be a great way to income split with a spouse or children. The building is purchased by the spouse and kids and then rented to the company at a hefty rate, thus creating a way to legally split income with a spouse or kids who may be in a lower marginal tax bracket.

Also with a purchase you have potential tax advantages through interest deductions & facility and equipment depreciation. If your company is large enough in size there can be local tax implications as well, as we have all seen over recent years with local state and provincial governments competing with each other to offer tax holidays to corporations to move their company to their respective jurisdictions.

Ownership in a good quality piece of property can also offer the corporation the possibility of a future sale-leaseback. This type of deal is typically only done by larger, well established, good credit risk type corporations. The sale-leaseback is a transaction where a company owns a piece of property but wants to free up some capital for whatever reason. The company sells the property to a non-related third party and then leases the property back for 10 or 20 years. The sale-leaseback can be a strategic move to free up capital that is tied up in real estate and provide a form of off balance sheet financing for specific projects or corporate objectives. It also frees

160

up lines of credit and other financing channels that corporations use.

As with all things in life there is a price to pay for these benefits.

First of all there is the sizable chunk of equity that is required to purchase a commercial property. There are, from time to time, government backed programs that enable you to get into a property with as little as 10% down but for the majority of the time the minimum investment required is in the 25 % to 35 % of purchase price range.

Secondly this is typically a long term investment and it is not the most liquid of investments. If the use or design of a property is very specific in nature due to the type of business that you have, it may be very difficult to sell the property when it comes time to get out. (Like my old boss used to say... be careful what you own because it ends up owning you.)

Of course as owner you are the go to guy when it comes to maintenance and repairs as well. Make sure you have funds set aside for emergencies and budget for long term capital items that wear out over time like furnaces, roofs, parking lots, sidewalk paving, etc.

Now let's look at Leasing.

Leasing commercial real estate can be attractive for many reasons.

First of all, leasing commercial real estate is the ultimate leverage for a business owner.

Think of it this way, if you have little money to invest it allows you to get a PREMIUM location for an easy monthly payment instead of the sizable investment that would be required to otherwise secure the very same location through a purchase. (If you could even buy it, as the most desirable locations are often NEVER for sale) Even if you do have a large chunk of cash you may still want to lease because the location that you can secure through leasing is still more desirable business wise than one you could secure through a purchase. This is why you see huge companies like Burger King, Wal-Mart, Sears, IKEA, etc. leasing space instead of buying. They have the cash to buy but it makes more business sense to lease in a better location.

You can also gain leverage through being able to find a location that was previously built out by someone else whose improvements to the space are still suitable for your needs. If you find a location that was fixed up by a previous Tenant and those improvements to the space still work for you with minimal change, you can save ten of thousands of dollars. Sometimes a Landlord would be willing to finish the space the way you need it and then amortize the costs of the improvements into the rent. Anytime you can get what you need for your business and not have to spend the money to get it that is a big benefit to your company.

Leasing is a an absolute boon to anybody looking to expand their business to multiple locations in a short time frame or anybody whose company is going through rapid growth. It can also allow you to keep the money in your business where it may be earning a higher rate of return than it could earn if it was invested in a piece of real estate.

Leasing provides flexibility to move with minimal time and expense at the end of a lease and depending on the Lease you sign, the ability to expand to adjacent space (if it is available) or shrink through sub-leasing as your company changes in size.

There are tax implications to leasing as well. You can deduct the full amount of the rent from your taxable income. Leasehold Improvements are capitalized and expensed over the life of the lease and the first two renewal options.

Some of the downsides to consider in leasing are as follows:

1. You future is affected by the decisions of others. If

your Landlord wants to raise your rents or not renew your lease it can have an immense impact on your business.

2. The money you spend each month does not create any long term wealth or asset value for you or your company.

3. Often the lease has clauses regarding the sale of your business to another person and the Landlord may have the right to reject any person whom you may be trying to sell your business to. Some leases even give the Landlord the right to terminate your lease if you try to sell your business or assign the lease to a new party. Read Your Lease Carefully and know how it will impact you!

So now that I have laid out the pros and cons to either option, here is the world as I see it. If your company is just starting out, is cash poor or is going through rapid changes in size due to growth or downsizing...Lease. If your company is mature, stable, experiencing slower growth patterns and is cash rich...Buy.

CHAPTER 40
WHAT IT TAKES TO SELL A HOUSE FAST IN TODAY'S FORECLOSURE SATURATED REAL ESTATE MARKET

In today's real estate market the challenge for homeowners who want to sell their home quickly is that they must compete with banks and other mortgage lenders who have taken back many homes via the foreclosure process. These foreclosed homes are then placed on the open market in a given community and are frequently being offered at eighty percent or less of their appraised value. This is having a significant downward effect on house prices. But, there are things you can do if you want to sell your house for cash today.

The residential real estate price challenge: Foreclosure homes weigh on market

America's housing market is currently staggering under a glut of unsold home inventory because of the biggest foreclosure crisis to hit the country since the Great Depression of the 1930's. There are many reasons why the country is in the middle of a foreclosure crisis, and other articles can provide the background for the downturn. Some topics to explore include: adjustable rate mortgages, subprime mortgages that swiftly became unaffordable, Alan Greenspan's Federal Reserve monetary policies, real estate speculation, and more.

This chapter explains some options available to a home seller to help them sell a house quickly even in a falling market whose bottom has not yet clearly been reached.

House selling option #1: Sell your house to a real estate investor

Homeowners who need to sell a house quickly because of unaffordable mortgage payments, job loss, transfer, or relocation, divorce, inheritance, or any other of number of reasons can look for a company that buys houses on the internet or via their local 'real estate wanted' section of their local newspaper to find a real estate investor who can buy a house for a cash offer in a short period of time. There are investors who advertise "we buy houses" on plastic signs on fences and telephone poles, but many of these signs are placed by investors of dubious backgrounds.

Do your homework on the internet if possible: make sure to research the person or company you are considering doing business with to see if they're reputable. If the investor claims to have professional licenses check their online records if available. In general, the 'simpler' the transaction the better chance you have of dealing with a straightforward purchaser. This means that you should sell the house directly and completely in the traditional formal manner at an escrow or title company of your choosing or with representation of an unbiased real estate attorney that is not working exclusively for the investor.

The upside of selling a home to a real estate investor for a cash purchase is that you can, if you meet certain criteria, walk away with cash in hand or a mortgage that will be paid off in a very short period of time. The downside is that investors will want to guarantee that they make a profit upon the resale of your house and their profit comes out of your equity in your home or your pocket.

Most real estate investors who buy single family homes and then re-sell them quickly (house flipping) and those who use a buy-and-hold strategy are looking for deep discounts on a home. This figure for an offer typically starts at 70% of current Fair Market Value (FMV). Of course most investors would prefer to purchase a home at far less than 70% of current FMV. There are some investors who will pay closer to 80% of current FMV for properties that they buy, but these buyers are difficult to locate at times. (Current FMV also means that a house's value is determined only after repair costs, if any, are subtracted.)

House selling option #2: "List Smart" with a real estate agent or broker

If you are the kind of home seller who wants to get top-dollar for your house, then this section may not give you the type of advice in terms of price you're looking for. But, if you're looking for a quick sale of your real estate read this article carefully and repeatedly.

The key to selling a house can be learned from the previous discussion of real estate investors' criteria for buying a house in terms of discount from current FMV. For your home to 'jump off the page' at a retail buyer if you have it listed with an agent or broker it must be priced significantly below the competition. It's really that simple. If your neighbor's identical house is listed for $210,000 and yours is priced at $195,000 whose home is going to be sold first?

Do you really want to be a FISBO and sell your house yourself?

For-sale-by-owner (FSBO) home selling strategies have always been popular in concept, and for people are sophisticated in terms of contract law, they can result in saving some money. But, for people with little experience buying and selling real estate the use of an experienced and licensed real estate professional can be an invaluable aid. Statistics published by the National Association of Realtors indicate that the typical FSBO home sold for $187,200 compared to $247,000 for agent-assisted home sales in 2007. Many do-it-yourself home sellers eventually sell or buy a home with the aid of an agent even if they have tried by themselves for a short or long while.

Create a real estate auction environment

You've probably seen the advertisements for real estate auctions in your area. Want to know the secret of how these auction companies stay in business? It's auction frenzy psychology.

By offering people looking to buy a home at an auction an opportunity to buy a foreclosed home at a very low price the auction companies are appealing to the greed of the bidders. Once this emotion of greed and a spirit of competition with the other buyers has kicked in many people will bid a price up on a home far in excess of the original asking price. An auction environment can definitely work against a buyer, especially if there are a lot of other bidders involved!

You can use this lesson to your advantage. If you price your home at an almost ridiculously low level you should expect to start receiving bids from potential buyers. Remember, it's better to have lots of low bidders, initially, that you can play off against each other and watch the price rise to close to the current fair market value or sometimes in excess of it. Also remember that you don't have to accept any offer you consider too low. Make sure you know the federal, state, and local laws that govern real estate law, contract law, and especially the non-discrimination provisions that apply.

House selling challenge #1: How to determine fair market value for my real estate

In today's real estate market determining the current FMV of a home is a very difficult thing to do. Most economists agree that home prices will continue to fall nationally for some time to come and that a true stabilization of US home prices may not occur for one to two years or more.

One quick and dirty to come up with a home's approximate FMV is to average the price that zillow.com and cyberhomes.com (and other online home appraisal sites) give to the house and then multiply that number by 85%. This should get you to a price that would make a retail home buyer or first-time home buyer jump at your house over the competition.

It is very, very important for home sellers to

170

understand the competitive landscape. Without a house priced at a deep discount from 'competitively' priced homes on the market a seller has little chance of getting top dollar or even any offers to purchase at all.

The only working definition of current fair market value that is worth remembering is that it is whatever a willing retail buyer will actually end up paying for your house in a 2 to 4 month period of time. These buyers, especially first-time homebuyers and people with less than perfect credit, are also facing their own challenges to qualify for a mortgage loan because of tighter underwriting standards imposed since the unfolding of the credit crisis in the United States.

House selling challenge #2: Low, no, or negative home equity

This is a tough situation and it's responsible for many of the foreclosures that are occurring in today's housing market. For people who purchased homes since 2003 (or even earlier) the chances are that their home does not have a lot of equity built up unless a substantial down payment was made on the house. For many of these homeowners who want to sell a home fast they are faced with an less than ideal situation of paying money at closing to sell their house to cover the amount they owe their mortgage lender in excess of the sales price and the closing costs.

When this can't happen because of limited financial resources on the seller's part the lender usually ends of taking the house back in foreclosure and it becomes part of the real estate owned (REO) inventory mentioned above that is acting as a drag on house values.

CHAPTER 41
HOW TO ATTRACT
MOTIVATED REAL ESTATE
SELLERS TO CALL YOU

I n science, as with all things in life, there are laws that govern how things work. For any endeavor, when you apply these laws, there will be identifiable results. It's no different with attracting success in real estate. There are Five Key Steps to becoming wealthy in real estate investing. These are very specific strategies that, if you follow them, will guarantee a successful return. If you have these five steps in order, you'll buy and sell 25 houses or more per year, and earn at least $500,000 a year, all while working 15 hours a week or less. The first step to follow is having Effective Marketing in place that attracts motivated house sellers. There are two ways this will happen:

They find you.

You approach them as a buyer.

Which way would be more efficient? Of course, it's much easier for them to call you as opposed to your labor in finding them. Additionally, when you are soliciting them, they are in control from a psychological point of view. You are demonstrating a need, and that puts them in a position to leverage that need.

We'll look at two low-cost, effective marketing mediums to attract motivated sellers to call you:

Newspaper Classified Ads (Real Estate Wanted Section-Daily)

Bandit Signs (Yard and/or Road Signs)

Classified Ads in the Real Estate Wanted Section

Run an ad daily in the Real Estate Wanted section of your local newspaper(s) 365 days a year. If your local newspaper doesn't have a Real Estate Wanted section, ask them to create one. If you tell them that you will be running an ad every single day, it'll be worth their effort. Also, this ad will buy more houses and definitely outweigh any cost that you initially put into it.

In some places, it costs $300 a month, and in other places it cost$1500 a month. Quite honestly, it doesn't matter what it costs. If you buy and sell just one house, that ad just paid for itself and then some. Here's what the ad should look like:

The first letter of each of these words is capitalized. Make sure you specify House in the first line and not Home. People are attached to homes, not houses, and we want people who want to get rid of their house. Do not capitalize everything because it's harder for the eyes to see. It is psychologically proven that when you only capitalize the first letter, and the rest of the letters are in normal type, it's much easier for eyes to capture when people are only looking at it for a second or two. This is proven marketing.

With numerous ads in the Real Estate Wanted section of the newspaper, how are house-sellers going to notice yours? Simple. Put a blank space at the top and bottom of the ad, so you're actually going to be paying for a six-line add, even though you only have words in the middle four lines. A reader's eyes will be drawn to that ad automatically. Your ad sticks out like a sore thumb.

Bandit Signs

The second most effective way to attract motivated sellers is bandit signs. These are the little road signs everyone's seen driving around. The signs should be yellow with black lettering, 18 inches high by 24 inches wide, and you want to use the entire space of the sign for the information to stand out. And they are going to come with a little wire stake. The bandit sign is going to say exactly the same thing as your classified ad.

The downside to bandit signs is that some towns and cities may have ordinances that don't allow them. You'll have to check your local laws to see if this applies to where you live. I suggest you still order 100 bandit signs, put them up, and if there's a problem, someone will let you know. You can claim ignorance, and you will definitely get a lot of calls from homeowners looking to sell. Bandit signs are worth the minimal risk.

Most people do not have the courage or the vision to put out the money to apply marketing strategies, and that's why they don't buy and sell houses, and make more money than they fear to lose. But one ad or bandit sign alone will get you at least 10 to 15 houses bought and sold per year, and it will save you the time and effort of going out and looking for prospects.

CHAPTER 42
REAL ESTATE INVESTMENT LOAN - TWO CRITICAL THINGS TO CONSIDER

Have you ever wondered why some real estate investors fail to meet their monthly bank instalments for their real estate investment loans or why their once stellar real estate investment has gone sour? This article will cover two critical external factors attributable to Real Estate Investment Loans that can affect the viability of your Real Estate Investment.

1. Interest Rates

One of the key advantages of Real Estate Investment over other types of investing is the ready access of information available through the traditional print media and the internet. If you do not know much about macro-economics, the first basic bit of economics that you can learn relating to your Real Estate Investment Loan, is the effect of an interest rate rise and whether there is going to be a rise and why and when. A rising interest rate may eat into your monthly cashflow and erode your earnings so it would be wise to spend some time thinking about the effect of a change in the interest rate on your current investment situation.

When choosing a Real Estate Investment Loan, you want to have an eye on current interest rates, future interest rates and the penalty that you might have to pay should you want to refinance your loan later to take advantage of a subsequently lower interest rate. So an obvious thing to do is to get a fixed interest rate, if you think that the interest rates are going to be higher in the next few months. The way to analyze this is to spend some time reading the business part of the newspapers to consider how monetary policy in the Federal Reserve is going to be in the next few months. This explains why some financial institutions and large property developers hire former Federal Reserve executives to tap on their expertise in understanding Federal Reserve Policy.

Another related interest rate investment strategy pertaining to Real Estate Investment Loans is to buy the property "subject to the existing mortgage" if the mortgage was locked in at a lower interest rate than the prevailing market rate. This particular strategy works well in a rising interest rate situation. Remember that a slight percentage increase may translate into a large jump in the amount of interest that you are paying so it would be wise to do your maths and get a friend to double check it before you leap into a deal.

178

2. Rental Yields

The most common indicator and thing that people would know about rental yield if you ask them is the Return on Investment (ROI). This is the annual rental as a percentage of the total cost of the property. So for example if I had paid $100,000 for the property and I recoup $10,000 per annum, my ROI would be 10%. Note that as a quick rule of thumb this also means that (excluding interest), you would fully pay up your property in ten years if you apply the full rental proceeds to servicing your real estate investment loan.

However, ROI is not the end all and be all of the analysis, another consideration when analyzing Rental Yield is not only the current or past rental yields but the future rental yields. Thus in order to do future projections, we need to study the property cycle of the target country and examine economic factors which may affect supply and demand of rental property in the area.

For example, let's say that we deem a particular Real Estate Investment viable this year for the purposes of cash flow and get a Real Estate Investment Loan. But what the you might have not considered is that you bought the property at a high in the property cycle and rental demand might go back to normal levels thereafter, rendering your so called Real Estate Investment in negative cash flow territory. So we can observe that you need to learn about the potential downside of your investment and do your sums carefully before you embark on getting your Real Estate Investment Loan.

Having a good understanding of interest rates and rental yields will enable you to profit from Real Estate Investment and as such it would be imperative to learn all you can about these things in your target market so as to maximize your profits and yields. Investing in property when viewed in this light can be said to be a science and it sometimes is best to treat it as such so as to remain detached when deciding on whether to enter into a deal.

CHAPTER 43
HOW TO BUY REAL ESTATE FOR PENNIES ON THE DOLLAR

REO Bank Foreclosures

Bank foreclosures are one of the more popular ways to buy real estate for pennies on the dollar. I have found that it's more like quarters on the dollar in most cases. There is a huge inventory and many resource with which to find bank owned properties. These are properties in which the buyer has defaulted on their mortgage and the bank has repossessed the property through foreclosure.

If you want to invest in these the first step is to figure out how to get enough of these deals coming across your desk to analyze. You will have to sift through quite a few to find the one that fit's within what you would consider to be pennies on the dollar (less than 50% market value). There are a bunch of REO websites online (Realtytrac is the main one I know of) and those are a good place to start.

Grabbing a realtor who specializes in REO's is another good tactic. This is good because they are familiar with the market, have access to the MLS, and are most likely skilled at short sale negotiation (short sales are basically when the bank will consider selling the property for less than what is owed). With those three hubs to your REO strategy you will have more than enough deals coming across your table.

Be careful not to accept just any deal. You may be tempted because it will seem like none of them are pennies on the dollar, or all the ones that are have already been taken. Do not fall into the temptation of getting into a contract for a property that is outside of your criteria. Understand what you want and stick to it. Communicate those wants to all involved. It will take time, but you will find what you're looking for.

Tax Foreclosures

In my opinion tax foreclosures present a better opportunity to buy real estate for pennies on the dollar. With tax foreclosures there is usually an upset sale, tax deed sale, or something of the sorts. This means that the local government, in order to settle the tax balance owed on the property, will perform an auction of that property to be sold for the amount of the taxes owed.

The good thing about this type of acquisition is that you will be able to truly buy real estate for pennies on the dollar. Sometimes you can buy a property for one tenth of it's actual market value. This gives more options to the investor because of the amount of built in equity. For example, the property acquired could be wholesaled to another investor at a price well below market and money is still made. For example, some counties in some states hold tax deed sales every month and the taxes owed on the property are sometimes under $10,000. The market value of these properties can be $40k - $100k in a lot of those cases. If you were able to acquire one of these properties for $10k and wholesale it to another investor for $15-$20k you would still make $5-$10k per month doing it. The other strategy is to sell it for the full market value once it is presentable. In the latter scenario you will hold onto the property longer and have more money invested in it, but will still make more money off the deal.

The challenges with this type of deal is that there are unknowns about the property we are buying. I, for example, bought one of these for $8,000 and later found out there were squatters in the house. A family was living there rent free, and I eventually had to go through an eviction process to get them out of there. One of the other challenges is getting clear title. It takes time to do this unless you have a system set up to expedite the process.

The title must be quieted and a quit claims deed will be issued once that process is successfully completed. A quieted title basically means that no one else can any longer establish rights to the property - including the previous owner. There are no encumbrances remaining after the procedure. There is a chance that someone will come back to claim the property, but they would have to pay you back the money for the property in order to reclaim it. This can only happen during the quiet title procedure period, which could be up to 90 days. To me, it is still a better deal than REO's, especially if you're willing to do your homework on prospective investment properties.

Tax Lien Certificates

Tax lien certificates allow you the best of two worlds. Not only can you potentially buy real estate for pennies on the dollar, but you can gain an interest income (tax free) if that doesn't happen.

Both tax liens and tax deeds are auctioned, but there are some differences between tax lien certificates and tax deed certificates. In essence, with tax lien certificates, we are loaning money to the municipality for taxes owed by the property owner. They, in turn, forward those interest charges to the property owner. If the taxes aren't collected after a certain period of time then the property is awarded to the lien holder. The interest gained on these certificates are tax free & the percentage of return can range from 10%-40% depending on where you are located. The money invested is tied up for a period of one to three years, also depending on where you are. This scenario is the worst case. You're money is tied up for three years and you gain 10%-40% interest on your money as a trade off.

The best case scenario is that you buy real estate for pennies on the dollar. You will get a property worth much more than you invested. A powerful strategy is to combine this tactic with a self directed, tax sheltered retirement account. You can develop your retirement money through this strategy (via Roth IRA) and have complete tax free gains and it's a very safe investment strategy.

The two downsides to this strategy is that it ties up your money and the investor is expected to pay the taxes in full within three days of the auction. If liquidity is a major part of your strategy then you'd need to steer clear of this one. This is a good strategy if you have a good amount of cash saved and don't mind having it tied up for a year or more.

Discount Mortgages

185

If you like income and growth strategies for investing then discount mortgages are a great strategy to buy real estate for pennies on the dollar. This is a cash flow strategy. Sometimes savvy investors, or home buyers, are able to negotiate flexible terms on a purchase. Sometimes these terms include a seller "holding paper" on the deal. This means that, instead of the buyer getting financing from a bank or other lender, the seller essentially becomes the lender on the home. The buyer will pay a mortgage to the seller instead of the bank and the seller will hold a lien on the property until that mortgage is paid off.

Unless you're in the cash flow business it can be unattractive to have someone paying you incremental payments for a home you wanted to sell outright. As a discount mortgage investor we can provide a solution. Usually we can offer a lump sum of cash for the payments being received by the seller. The lump sum we offer is normally 70% or less of what the face value of the note is. Time value of money is a big factor with these discounts. I suggest not paying more than 60% if the note is high quality.

A high quality note is one that has a buyer with an excellent payment history, good credit and a stable income. The benefits of doing this are (1) we can pretty much pick the rate of return we want to receive on this investment and (2) if things go south we could end up with a property worth much more than we have in it. This also is a good retirement strategy because it could be a source of income for us later on, if we decide to hold onto these good performing notes*. Just like in tax lien certificates it would be powerful to combine this with an tax sheltered retirement account.

The downside of discount mortgages, like tax lien certificates, is liquidity. It provides a monthly cash flow but it ties our principle up for a good amount of time. There are transfer/assignment options for the note, but most likely the face value would take a hit if we were to cash out to another investor. This is a longer term strategy. We must be comfortable receiving the cash flow in return for the lump sum. Also, to be in this business we need to do our homework to understand the finance behind the strategy (future value, time value, interest, etc.).

Distressed Properties (Motivated Sellers)

This is a buy real estate for pennies on the dollar strategy that requires some keen negotiation skills, and some bird dogging. Finding distressed properties is an art in and of itself. There must be a system for locating these, otherwise the deals will be too few and far between. A distressed property is a property that has been abandoned, run down, sitting on the market for too long, or has an owner with personal issues that cause them not to be able to deal with the property at the present time.

The good thing about these kind of properties is that we can sometimes get them at a great discount. More often than not, though, it will be hard to gain a discount of 50% or more. The other thing to be aware of is that there will be a lot of work involved in cases such as abandoned homes, run down properties, and other such fixer uppers if we are looking to capitalize on the full equity. Wholesaling, and bird-dogging are good strategies for those who don't wish to put that type of time into it. Bird-doggers can find these properties and flip them to other investors for a finders fee.

I've found it more difficult to accomplish a win-win negotiation with sellers in these situations. When it comes down to it they want to sell the property to get their money, and my goal is to get the property for pennies on the dollar. The key here is to identify seller who are motivated by other reasons and focus on those as opposed to the money. For example, they may be living far away from the property, have had a hard time selling, and no longer want to deal with traveling back and forth or continuing to pay money for taxes and maintenance. In this situation we can focus on the time & money they will save from us taking it off of their hands. This is a good

188

strategy for someone who is handy, or has a good network.

How to Buy Real Estate for Pennies on the Dollar (Summary)

Robert Kiyosaki points out that we make money when we buy. Using any, or a combination of these strategies will help us to do just that. Built in equity is the ultimate goal when investing in real estate, for me. Other people have different goals for real estate investing such as tax deferment, depreciation and other such tax strategies, as well as wealth building with the expectation that the property value is going to rise. These are okay strategies as well. I tend to like to buy real estate for pennies on the dollar because, to me, it provides greater protection from risk. There is a lot of built-in equity with which to work. I hope this discussion is as beneficial to you as it is to me.

CHAPTER 44
HOW QUICK TURN REAL ESTATE CAN MAKE YOU RICH - THE ART AND SCIENCE OF 'REHAB AND RETAIL'

A quick turn real estate business helps you make money fast...and without a lot of headaches. You can work from home, work part time, and even get started in real estate investing without a big chunk of upfront capital. No wonder quick turn real estate is one of the fastest growing segments in the real estate investing arena.

Generally speaking, there are five ways you can profit from quick turn real estate transaction strategies. In this chapter, I want to tell you about one of them. It's a basic of real estate investing, and it's commonly referred to as "rehab and retail."

In quick turn real estate, when you buy a house at a low cost and sell it for a higher amount, it's called retailing. You purchase a house 'wholesale,' perhaps do some modest repairs, and then sell it for a profit. What kinds of profits are we taking about in quick turn real estate? How much you earn will depend on whether you're working full or part-time and on how many houses you sell. The average profit per sale is $20,000 to $35,000. In real estate investing...those are good numbers!

In this regard, real estate investing is similar to any business where you mark up the price of an item before offering it for sale. And just like any other business, it can fail.

As well as being one of the most popular ways to profit from quick turn real estate, rehab and retail is also one of the most profitable. Yet despite the money that can be made this way, rehab-and-retail continues to be one of the most misunderstood techniques in real estate investing. Although the process sounds simple - buy, repair, sell - the reality of rehab and retail transactions is quite different. There are many costly problems that can arise with rehab and retail, especially during the repair process. For this reason, I recommend that novice investors choose another quick turn real estate investment strategy.

Does that mean I'm saying that your real estate investing business should never focus on rehab and retail? Not at all. In fact, if you really enjoy home renovation and really get a kick out transforming a fixer-upper into a 'castle,' then you may be very well suited to the demands of rehab and retail.

If that's the direction you'd like to go in, let me offer you these

Top 4 Tips For Doing Well with Rehab and Retail Transactions

Location, Location, Location - Limit your purchases to areas where qualified buyers will want to live. No matter how well you renovate, it's going to be tough to sell a home in a high crime area. Why take unnecessary risks? Stick to better neighborhoods for your real estate investing.

Assume Nothing - Under no circumstances (that means NEVER) close on a property until you have had it appraised and assessed by professionals (contractors, service people, etc.) so that you know what repairs are required, what those repairs will cost, and what the home will be worth (repaired value) when the work is complete.

Expect the Unexpected - Inevitably, home repairs will take longer and cost more than anticipated. It's one of the biggest downsides of this quick turn real estate strategy. Be sure to borrow enough to cover more than just the purchase price and the estimated repair costs to give yourself a 'cash reserve' to fall back on.

Trust No One - I know this sounds harsh, but

contractors, on site workers, and others involved in home renovation are notorious for bad business practices. Get recommendations from people you know, if possible. Supervise the work and keep a close eye on progress and the bottom line.

CHAPTER 45
HOW TO USE REAL ESTATE CYCLES TO YOUR ADVANTAGE AS AN INVESTOR

Recently, there have been events within the real estate market that have caused many markets to change. These changes affected many real estate investors because the investors were not adjusting their strategy to the market. When the market changes as it has, your investing strategy must change as well.

You will be able to use this chapter to help you identify stages in the real estate cycle. When you know what the stages are in the cycle and what is causing the change, it will be easier for you to see the next stage coming. As a result, you can tailor your investing strategy to what is happening in your market.

Real Estate Cycle Stages

When you look at real estate cycle, the stages of the cycle go like this:

1. Increasing Rents/Prices

2. Increasing Construction

3. Overbuild

4. Rent Concessions

5. Declining Rents/Prices

6. High Vacancy

7. Little Activity

8. Accumulation

9. Low Vacancy

10. Increasing Rents/Prices (and the cycle continues on)

Basically, the factors affecting these cycles all revolve around simple supply and demand factors. Supply and demand are the major influences how the cycle changes from one stage to the next. Let's start with Increasing Rents/Prices portion of the cycle. The demand has outpaced the supply and caused prices to go up.

As supply begins to catch up with demand, the cycle goes towards the bottom of the cycle which is declining rents/prices. Listed above are the stages that happen between the top and bottom of the cycle. The important thing to remember is that supply (existing homes for sale/rent and new construction) and demand (people wanting homes for purchase/rent) is what is driving the changes in the cycle.

Keep in mind that there is not a set time frame of how long it takes to go from one stage of the cycle to the next. It could take 20 years or more to go around the cycle one time. It is also important to point out that each real estate market acts independently based on the supply and demand of their own area. This means that New York, Houston, and Seattle are all going to be in different stages of the cycle because they are their own market.

From my experience of training investors, we have found that there are certain investing techniques that are more effective in one stage of the cycle than another. In the top portion of the cycle (this means starting with the little activity stage and going around the cycle until the overbuild stage) rentals, rehabbing, and lease options are the best strategies that are suited for those conditions. These strategies will help you take advantage of the increasing demand to maximize your profits based on strategies that benefit from the increasing demand.

In the bottom portion of the cycle (starting with the overbuild stage and continuing until little activity) wholesaling, seller financing, and lease options are usually the best strategies for those stages of the cycle. Lease options mainly work well in the bottom stages of the cycle as an entrance strategy so that you are not stuck with a deal that is declining in value. These strategies are designed to protect you from the downside of the market while being able to profit.

What Does This All Mean?

The purpose of this chapter is to keep people from making mistakes when buying investment real estate. When investors understand how cycles work, what is driving the cycles, and what techniques are best, their success rate increases dramatically. You will be investing with the trends of the market instead of fighting against it. You are not going to be able to change the market conditions, but you can use techniques that will put market conditions in your favor. This is truly becoming an investor as you use the market to your advantage.

If you know what stage your market is in, you will also be able to adjust your strategy as the market changes. When you see levels of supply and demand changing, you can prepare for the next market cycle and modify your strategy to match the conditions. I am not telling you to time the market. Trying to time the market usually ends up in disaster. What I am telling you is that money can be made in real estate at any time. It is a matter of knowing how to use various techniques and when to use them. This will make your success rate increase because you will be able to make a profit when other investors cannot.

Critical Steps

Whenever you consider purchasing an investment property, I recommend the following steps:

1. Identify the stage of the cycle in your market - Again this will be based on supply (inventory of properties for sale/rent/being built) and demand (people moving in, jobs coming in, number of properties being sold). Find a qualified real estate agent and your city planner to obtain this information.

2. Analyze the deal - You need to crunch the numbers to ensure that the deal is profitable. Is there a certain technique you are going to use on the deal?

3. Make sure the technique works well for that stage of the cycle - When you align the market stage, the property, and the strategy with your market conditions, profitable deals are much easier to do. Successful deals are more plentiful when all three of these factors are aligned.

Spend the necessary time to obtain the information on your real estate market. This information will make you a more powerful investor so that you do not get stuck in deals that are not good for your market conditions

CONCLUSION

It is sometimes better to have a month to month lease with your rental real estate investment. The benefits far outweigh the costs, and certain good tenants would prefer the shorter terms. The short time length allows you to get any undesirable or non paying tenants out a lot faster, so good tenants can be found and moved in. This can save you quite a bit of money, repairs, and hassles. You invested in real estate to protect your money and make it grow, and a shorter lease period will work harder for your money.

A short sale is a sale of real estate in which the sale proceeds fall short of the balance owed on the property's loan and is a strategy rapidly gaining popularity in the real estate market. It is a real estate transaction in which the seller's lender agrees a payoff that is less than the balance due on the loan and in which the borrower does not have to pay the difference. This agreement takes place between the seller and their lender, prior to the onset of foreclosure, allowing the home to be sold for less than the current outstanding loan balance. When a homeowner owes more on their home than it is worth, this type of sale may be an option. The goal of a short sale is to help the homeowner avoid foreclosure and when both the borrower and the lender agree to the process, it generally enables the avoidance of foreclosure, which involves hefty fees for the bank and poorer credit report outcomes for the borrowers. Keep in mind that, unlike bankruptcy line items, short sales do show on a credit report and can remain on your credit report for 7-10 years.

A real estate investor engaging for the first time in foreclosures and short sales will need to know exactly what such a transaction is and clearly understand the process involved. A key component for a buyer to be successful when purchasing a short sale is to make sure that they do research on the market conditions and area of the home. Although acquisition through this type of deal structure can be a successful strategy in purchasing distressed real estate, due to the real estate market's foreseeable inconsistencies a buyer can purchase a home and still experience additional reduction in value. Keep in mind that while Lenders want to get rid of distressed properties as soon as possible, they typically aren't going to sell them for ridiculously low prices. It is also important to remember that it is very possible that a transaction can and will fall through if the Broker Price Opinions come in much higher than the agreed upon price.

A real estate short sale is a strategy that can help homeowners who owe more for their house than the houses are worth, and is another option of relief for troubled homeowners. Before proceeding with any real estate deal it is imperative to evaluate your personal situation and determine if the proposed contract and property is right for you. A short sale is typically faster and less expensive than a foreclosure, but there are downsides that merit consideration as well. Sellers should be careful to consult with their lenders and tax advisers as to the impact of any financial event of this magnitude and clearly understand the impact of the potential outcomes. If all other options have been exhausted and a short sale is the best choice, it is highly recommended that the seller work with a licensed real estate agent who can assist in listing the home for sale. Sellers should also keep in mind that Buyers can get tired of waiting for the sale approval and cancel because banks can't currently process these types of deals fast enough. Buyers need to understand the current market conditions and values and work with a Realtor they trust. However, when utilized in the appropriate situations a short sale can be beneficial to all parties involved.

REFERENCES

https://thecollegeinvestor.com/16399/20-passive-income-ideas/

https://www.creditdonkey.com/passive-income.html

https://www.pulse.ng/bi/finance/a-self-made-millionaire-who-retired-at-30-says-the-2-best-ways-to-build-long-term/n6drpvr

The forex world 1992 Odufuwa Seyi

https://www.dollarsprout.com/passive-income-ideas/

The wiled fund Thomas Thomas Edison

https://www.forbes.com/sites/jrose/2019/02/07/passive-income-ideas-2019/

Statistics published by the national association of realtors 2007

How to buy real estate for pennies on the dollar, Robert Kiyosaki

https://www.bankrate.com/investing/passive-income-ideas/

Do not go yet; One last thing to do

If you enjoyed this book or found it useful I'd be very grateful if you'd post a short review on it. Your support really does make a difference and I read all the reviews personally so I can get your feedback and make this book even better.

Thanks again for your support!